WORLD-BUILDERS ON WORLD-BUILDING

With contributions from a distinguished group of world-builders, including academics, writers, and designers, this anthology of essays describes the process and discusses the nature of subcreation and the construction of worlds.

From Oz to MUD, *Walden* to Rockall, all the worlds featured in this volume share one thing in common: they began in someone's imagination, grew from there, and became worlds built with the assistance of multiple authors and a variety of different ideas and media, including designs, imagery, sound, music, stories, and more. The book examines this development, with examples and discussions pertaining to the process and the final product of the building of imaginary worlds, including some transmedial worlds.

World-Builders on World-Building is a fascinating deep dive into the practical problems of world-building as well as its theoretical aspects. It is ideal for students, scholars, and even practitioners interested in media studies, game studies, subcreation studies, franchise studies, transmedia studies, and pop culture.

Mark J. P. Wolf is a Professor in the Communication Department at Concordia University Wisconsin. His 23 books include *The Video Game Theory Reader 1* and *2* (2003, 2008), *The Video Game Explosion* (2007), *Myst & Riven: The World of the D'ni* (2011), *Before the Crash: Early Video Game History* (2012), *Encyclopedia of Video Games* (2012), *Building Imaginary Worlds* (2012), *The Routledge Companion to Video Game Studies* (2014), *LEGO Studies* (2014), *Video Games Around the World* (2015), *Revisiting Imaginary Worlds* (2016), *Video Games FAQ* (2017), *The World of Mister Rogers' Neighborhood* (2017), *The Routledge Companion to Imaginary Worlds* (2017), *The Routledge Companion to Media Technology and Obsolescence* (2018), which won the SCMS 2020 award for best edited collection.

WORLD-BUILDERS ON WORLD-BUILDING

An Exploration of Subcreation

Edited by Mark J. P. Wolf

Routledge
Taylor & Francis Group

NEW YORK AND LONDON

First published 2020
by Routledge
52 Vanderbilt Avenue, New York, NY 10017

and by Routledge
2 Park Square, Milton Park, Abingdon, Oxon, OX14 4RN

Routledge is an imprint of the Taylor & Francis Group, an informa business

Library of Congress Cataloging-in-Publication Data
Names: Wolf, Mark J. P., editor.
Title: World-builders on world-building : an exploration of subcreation /
    edited by Mark J.P. Wolf.
Description: New York, NY : Routledge, 2020. | Includes bibliographical
    references and index.
Identifiers: LCCN 2020002650 (print) | LCCN 2020002651 (ebook) |
    ISBN 9780367197254 (hardback) | ISBN 9780429242861 (ebook)
Subjects: LCSH: Creation (Literary, artistic, etc.) | Imaginary societies.
Classification: LCC PN56.C69 W68 2020 (print) | LCC PN56.C69
    (ebook) | DDC 809/.922—dc23
LC record available at https://lccn.loc.gov/2020002650
LC ebook record available at https://lccn.loc.gov/2020002651

ISBN: 978-0-367-19725-4 (hbk)
ISBN: 978-0-429-24286-1 (ebk)

Typeset in Bembo
by Apex CoVantage, LLC

A. M. D. G.

CONTENTS

ACKNOWLEDGMENTS

An anthology like this is only possible because of all the people who enjoy writing about, reading about, and building imaginary worlds, and I am grateful to see this interdisciplinary area of study increasing in academia over the years. I would like to thank production designer Alex McDowell for his Foreword and for all the work he has done to advance world-building in cinema. A hearty thanks go to all of the essay contributors, Richard A. Bartle, Clara Fernández-Vara, Tracy Fullerton, Henry Jenkins, Mark R. Johnson, Mark Sebanc, and Matthew Wiese, for their participation and great essays and for the online conversations we have had regarding imaginary worlds. I am also grateful for the enthusiasm and encouragement of Erica Wetter and Emma Sherriff at Routledge and the anonymous book proposal reviewers for their thoughtful and thorough reviews. Thanks also to my wife, Diane, and my sons, Michael, Christian, and Francis, who put up with me during the time I was working on this book. And, as always, thanks be to God, the Creator of all subcreators.

FOREWORD

The Zone, and the Instruments of Building a World

World-Builders on World-Building gathers deep thinkers from the diverse worlds of world-building. Every essay in this book has at its core the intelligence, breadth, and depth of a holistic world. Inside each world is a foundation that is essential but often hidden. When unearthed, it reveals a system that just begins to convey the complexity of the narratives that evolve from it.

Any world worth its salt is unbounded.

To ideate, prototype, develop, and understand the complexity of a world within any practical constraints, we must be able to enter it before it exists. A world changes constantly because we change our viewpoints and vectors constantly. We need to develop the knowledge, depth, and complexity for a multidimensional structure that can support our stories. The intended world is too intricate to understand, yet we cannot understand it unless we begin to build it.

We can know a street corner, a plant, or a machine intimately. We understand their narrative and materials, the function of their moving parts, and how they represent a larger order. Each of these can be epitomized through the trope of a Zone.

A Zone can be sculpted by the intricate collaboration of its creators to become a micro-representation of the holistic world – filled with intimate stories that correlate with the larger narratives. A Zone exists in time and space. There is decay and growth, transaction and trade, food consumed and bicycles ridden, crime and misbehavior, governance and infrastructure, water flowing, and the constant movement of people within and woven through its expanse. It has infrastructure, opinion, economy, tools, fuel, smells, weather. It mirrors the macro-system world.

Alongside its uniquely variable characteristics, a Zone is defined by fluidity, the movement through it, and its flow through time. Each Zone becomes a multilayered and orbital representation of a greater world, with much of the depth and detail of the world contained in the smallest possible space. It is a powerful tool.

[pause]

Despite the augmentation of our human capabilities through new technologies that now seem to define our process, the instruments of our storytelling remain sadly inadequate. We want to create a container of narratives that are as chaotic and finely detailed as walking into a busy street, or a forest, but, like an architect's vision, we can never achieve the structure that was perfectly formed when it was first imagined.

We are not equipped to transmit a world that is defined by limitless imagination when our woven narratives are still constrained by process. We want to make an empathetic connection between the fabric and the wearer that becomes deeper through time and broader through space, but we don't have the means to fashion it. This failure is not defined by granularity or level of detail; it's defined by believability, and to live in these worlds is to suspend our disbelief.

Historically, from the first spark of an idea, we have not been able to confront the scale of the system it will provoke, so either we imagine the whole world first, as a shell to be filled, or we initiate an author's vision to conjure a world through a narrative thread. In either case, we have built answers, not questions.

But imagine that the system itself is the driver of the world. Because its rhizomatic development is by default chaotic, one has to define its rules before the world is formed. And so we return to the Zone, where the system is evolving under a microscope, but as a mirror of the whole, and where the rules can be seen unfolding until they plateau. And at each step of the way questions are raised, and the interrogation continues as the logic of the world unfolds. Every part of the machinery gradually becomes self-motivated; each system is an adaptive organism that we can trigger into existence by just a single provocation. The key to this statement is *we*. Every world is the product of collaboration between experts, designers, developers, scientists, and the world itself. There is no single author. These worlds are not set; no boundless world ever ends or evolves as it was conceived.

The key to knowing the whole of a world is to know the street corners, plants, machines, and human organisms at its center. The Zone allows us to enter the world that does not yet exist, observe it as it is formed, and participate in its holistic development into maturity, unyielding in its logic, but fluid and unbounded.

Alex McDowell
December 15, 2019

INTRODUCTION

Many of the activities I did when I was young – playing with LEGO, drawing maps, coming up with stories, writing video games for my TI99/4a computer (mostly adventure games), taking architecture in high school, film production and animation in college, and writing two novels (still unpublished) – I only later realized all had a common theme to them: world-building. This tendency also affected many of my media-consumption choices: the novels I read, movies I watched, video games I most enjoyed, and so on. And I was not alone; growing up in the 1970s, there were many fans of Tolkien's work, which was becoming widely known (and which received even more recognition when *The Silmarillion* was published in 1977), and his work inspired tabletop games like *Dungeons & Dragons* (1974) and role-playing games in general, as well as a myriad of fantasy authors whose works and worlds debuted during that decade. *Star Wars* (also 1977) was a groundbreaking film in the area of cinematic world-building and led to more science-fiction films and universes (including the resurrection of *Star Trek* as a feature-length motion picture in 1979) as well as television shows with their own universes, like *Battlestar Galactica* (1978–1979). Video games began appearing in the arcade and the home, offering worlds which one could vicariously enter and explore, growing from text and simple graphics to more elaborate worlds over the years. By the late 1970s and into the 1980s, the importance of worlds as an advertising and marketing tool became more apparent, and greater efforts were made in the franchising and merchandising of worlds.

The period also saw more world-building possibilities open up for the public. Although self-publishing had always been around – including authors like Laurence Sterne, Jane Austen, Walt Whitman, Marcel Proust, Virginia Woolf, and others – it was in 1979 when desktop publishing, made possible by the arrival of digital technology, began to change the world of publishing and open up new venues for authors and world-builders. Home computer systems let users program their own games, while home video cameras made home moviemaking less expensive. Starting as ARPAnet in 1969, the Internet also grew up in the 1970s, first as an all-text medium and, along with bulletin board systems (BBSs) in the 1980s, began to bring together groups of people with similar interests, including fan clubs devoted to various imaginary worlds and their authors as well as people interested in world-building itself. And, of course, when the graphical user interface (GUI) of the Internet appeared in 1993, in the form of the World Wide Web, the Internet became a publishing medium as well.

Along with all the new worlds, a greater interest in world-building, and venues for amateur world-builders, came more tools for world-building. From the 1980s onward, "how-to" books on world-building would appear, and tools like Mark Rosenfelder's *Language Construction Kit* (1998) were designed to aid world-building activities. While such books and tools might demystify the world-building process, their suggestions made the process less idiosyncratic and were perhaps partly responsible for a number of standardized, cookie-cutter worlds lacking the uniqueness of the famous imaginary worlds that inspired them. At the same time, however, they had the potential of making people more aware of world-building processes and perhaps even more critical of the worlds they encountered. With the rise of the Internet and especially the World Wide Web, authors – whether published, self-published, or unpublished – could put up their own websites and communicate with readers and fellow world-builders. Communication between authors and fans in which the comments of the latter could shape the worlds of the former had occurred as early as the days of L. Frank Baum and Edgar Rice Burroughs, but it was not until the rise of websites that such communication, along with discussion fora that authors could follow, would become commonplace.

Since the 1990s, digital video–editing software, Photoshop and other image-editing software, and computer animation programs have provided even more tools for world-builders, both amateur and professional. As many fan films and user-made videos on YouTube and elsewhere have demonstrated, high-quality world-building can be done even in one's spare time, albeit usually in much smaller doses than in the commercial cinema. And starting with computer programs like Silicon Beach Software's *World Builder* (1986) for the Apple Macintosh, game creation programs have developed, along with game engines and modding, allowing the construction of game worlds to become easier for users, even those of virtual reality, as the technology becomes more common and construction programs become available. Practically every type of world-building is now available to the public as well as the industry, and sometimes used by both.

Of course, world-building involves far more than just the familiarity and use of world-building programs or tools. As in any art, coming up with something meaningful and original has always been – and will always be – a challenge, along with the incarnating of ideas into concrete descriptions, images, and sounds. While many worlds are well known, the methods behind their creation are less known, though more "making of" books, featurettes, and videos have been available than ever. Most of these, too, tend to be more about the steps in a world's evolution (early sketches and ideas, designs proposed and rejected, and so forth) than the actual processes used to come up with worlds or to hone and build them. The essays in this book give a few examples of such things and are discussions not just of worlds but of world-building itself, both theory and practice.

As a follow-up to my books *Building Imaginary Worlds: The Theory and History of Subcreation* (Routledge, 2012), *Revisiting Imaginary Worlds: A Subcreation Studies Anthology* (Routledge, 2017), and *Exploring Imaginary Worlds: Essays in Media, Structure, and Subcreation* (Routledge, forthcoming), this book comes at the topic from a different angle, from the point of view of the world-builder. In fact, this book was originally part of the *Exploring Imaginary Worlds* anthology, until the press suggested that it become a separate book, since a number of the essays were more about the process of world-building than just exploring existing worlds. So we separated them; I added a few more essays; and in the end, it was a good idea, as it really is a different focus. If, instead of just visiting imaginary worlds, you have actually tried building one yourself, your outlook changes. You begin to realize the requirements are more than that of a typical story set in the Primary World (which is itself no easy thing to create well, either), and you've got to find out things like the history of your world; its aesthetics; the feel of the place overall and the different, individual places within it; and all the details that give it the life that it should have – the sense of something ongoing that continues to exist with life going on there even when we aren't watching it.

As the appendix to the book discusses, people can world-build and be world-builders to differing degrees. Some might originate new worlds; while others might work on specific parts of worlds or the audience's experience of those worlds; and some might even adapt, update, or expand an older world for audiences of today. The essays in the book are arranged in roughly the chronological order of the appearances of their worlds, and the first essay looks at how a world over a century old – L. Frank Baum's world of Oz and its surrounding lands – is being updated for children's television of the 21st century. In "'Matter, Dark Matter, Doesn't Matter': An Interview with *Lost in Oz*'s Bureau of Magic", Henry Jenkins interviews some of the world-builders working on the show, and the process of transformation involved. An in the case of *Lost in Oz*, there's much more going on than just adaptation and transformation, as a great deal of new material and ideas are being developed, visualized, and integrated into the world.

The visualization of a world can also be done through words, and the next essay, Richard A. Bartle's "The Making of *MUD*: Three Stories of Genesis" describes Bartle's building of the first MUD, which stands for multi-user dungeon (or domain), the predecessor of today's online worlds and massively multiplayer online role-playing games (MMORPGs), and considers its genesis in three different ways. Authors can carry on the work of others, and Mark Sebanc's essay "Rockall: A Liminal, Transauthorial World Founded on the Atlantis Myth" concerns his work on the world of William Antony Swithin Sarjeant's world of Rockall, after Sarjeant's death.

Video games have now become a popular venue for world-building and are the subject of the next three essays. "Making Worlds Into Games – a Methodology" by Clara Fernández-Vara and Matthew Wiese is a detailed explanation of the world-building processes employed by the authors during the making of video games, and they have also taught these processes to their students, leading them to consider how the teaching of world-building might be done. Tracy Fullerton's essay "Surveying the Soul: Creating the World of *Walden, a Game*" discusses her inspiration and work on a game which recreates Thoreau's experiences at Walden Pond, creating a contemplative experience for players. And Mark R. Johnson's essay, "The Place of Culture, Society, and Politics in Video Game World-Building", describes his ongoing work on *Ultima Ratio Regum*, a game which will have procedurally generated cultures and algorithmic world-building.

Finally, my own essay "Concerning the 'Sub' in 'Subcreation': The Act of Creating Under" explores just how far a secondary world can be from resembling the Primary World in some way: how different can it be, how many Primary World defaults can it change, and what happens when those defaults are changed?

Considering the efforts required to build an imaginary world (at least one detailed enough to be immersive), it is perhaps not surprising that so many authors of imaginary worlds have written about building them as well, seeing as putting theory into practice often develops one's notions of the theory along with the building of a world. With all the established imaginary world conventions and traditions, along with a plethora of new world-building tools to help speed up, automate, and track the process of world-building, there is more world-building activity and discussion of it than ever before.

1

"MATTER, DARK MATTER, DOESN'T MATTER"

An Interview With *Lost in Oz*'s Bureau of Magic

Henry Jenkins

Few fictional worlds have received as much scholarly and fan attention as L. Frank Baum's Oz, and with good reason.[1] Fashioning himself as the Royal Historian of Oz, Baum himself wrote 14 books set in Oz and further expanded it through comic strips, stage plays, films, and traveling lectures, among other media.[2] Subsequent authors added another 55 authorized books in the series. And, of course, the books have been adopted and extended through live action and animated films, television specials and series, games, comic books, and revisionist novels through the years.

Following in this rich tradition, *Lost in Oz*, an animated serial about a contemporary Dorothy who finds herself in an updated version of the Emerald City, launched as a movie on Amazon in 2016 and as a series in 2017. So far, the Bureau of Magic, the creative team behind the series, has produced two seasons representing 26 episodes. I was invited to serve as an advisor for the series, helping them work through the connections with the larger Oz story world, explore potential entry points for transmedia extensions, and discuss the pedagogical implications of their creative choice.

I was able to sit down with *Lost in Oz*'s executive producers, Abram Makowka, Darin Mark, Jared Mark, and Mark Warshaw, for a conversation about world-building in May 2019. The close-knit creative team members were completing each other's sentences and building on each other's ideas through the interview which often suggested the feel of a brainstorming session. Along the way, they gave me a sense of the multiple levels on which they thought about Oz as a fictional realm within which to set their series, moving quickly between visual and narrative elements as understood in relation to audience expectations, programming strategies, and budget constraints that shaped the production process. As such, this interview speaks to many issues which have concerned theorists and critics interested in world-building and world-sharing in the contemporary American entertainment industry.

Why Oz?

Henry Jenkins: So, what makes Oz a great intellectual property?

Mark Warshaw: I'd start with a character, Dorothy Gale, that is relatable and somehow timeless, helping kids find their way into this fantasy world. She gives us familiar eyes to look through as we see all this incredible stuff.

Darin Mark: But that said, it's worth noting that in the books, Dorothy is a much more passive protagonist than our version of Dorothy.

Rule number one was creating a lead female character that has agency and makes bold choices, makes mistakes, and suffers her own consequences. So, right from the opening scenes of *Lost in Oz*, it's Dorothy's curiosity and her inability to let a problem go unsolved that triggers this entire journey, whereas originally Dorothy's trip to Oz was a bit more haphazard than that.

Mark Warshaw: But to your question, L. Frank Baum built this amazing architecture into the original canon. We can now – this many years later – go back and adapt Baum's vision for a new generation. We never wanted to just tell the story that he told. We wanted to embrace his story, learn from it, and then springboard off of it to create an Oz for a modern audience.

Jared Mark: At its foundation, it's a story about somebody going far from home, far from her comfort zone, to a world she's never experienced before, as a complete outsider. And once there, she embraces the singular mission of trying to go home again.

But along the way, Dorothy meets all of these other characters and all of these other creatures that had their own problems to solve. The original Dorothy makes some of those problems her own. And so, now, she's trying to solve her problem, but she's also trying to help others along the way. For the modern character, she gets herself into this predicament, gets herself far from home.

Why tell the story today? Here's a story about going as far away from your home, as far away from your comfort zone as you could possibly get, and still having the wherewithal and the kindness to take on other people's problems, form a community, and find a sense of purpose and place. And then to bring all of that knowledge back with you.

Abram Makowka: You will find that by mid-second season, Oz is starting to feel more like home, and she has greater ambivalences about whether she wants to stay there or not.

Jared Mark: She gets into the entire notion of what makes home a home, and that becomes a real touchstone for us, "Is home a place? A people? A feeling? What makes a home?"

Mark Warshaw: This world that Baum set up doesn't have many rules. And as it goes deeper and deeper into the books, Baum is making things up as he goes along. So, the possibilities are endless. Baum offers us this rich fertile ground to play in.

And so, we took all those books and said, "That's canon and that happened", but then we take Geoffrey Long's idea of negative space.[3]

[Editor's Note: Long writes that negative space refers to "some parts of the story deliberately untold" so that it allows the reader to speculate and "fill in those gaps for themselves". In this case, Warshaw suggests that future creators may also build on negative space in order to expand the fictional world so that it can yield new stories that address a new generation of readers and viewers.]

Baum left us plenty of room within Oz where we can pick up the story.

And as we started to weave the world together, we are taking the stuff that was originally there and speculating about what it would become today. What would happen if Dorothy went to Oz today? And by starting to answer that question, we began to build up the world where our story takes place.

Reimagining the Land of Oz

Henry Jenkins: So, let's build on that. How do you think about Oz today as opposed the Oz that would have existed 100-plus years before? How did you think about updating Oz?

Mark Warshaw: We thought about the impact of people who have traveled to and from this world before, starting with the original Dorothy whose visit to Oz is now a historical event in our story. She's now one of multiple visitors from our world who influenced this time line. So, what inventions did they bring into this world? What aspects of our world would have influenced the growth and evolution of the Oz of today?

We wanted to turn the Emerald City into a big metropolis and make it look like a city that kids growing up today may have visited or actually lived in. This was a piece of concept art that our team in Scotland created [Figure 1.1]. When we saw

FIGURE 1.1 Emerald City concept art

this, this clicked as what Emerald City and the world of our show would look like.

We wanted that vibrancy and that kinetic energy: our Oz would be a bustling place that felt like a mix of Hong Kong or Tokyo or New York City. You take that, and you tether back to what Baum really laid [out] in his original Emerald City. We talked a lot about the different cultures, right?

Jared Mark: Absolutely. What's in the books happened, the characters in the canon existed. All that is history in this world. And we are now 100 years out from that. Well, let's imagine what's happened to the populations, to the geography, to the demographics of this world.

We said, "What if we started with that circular city that Baum designed – the four quadrants? What if we expand from there and urban sprawls started happening?" And so, that area has gotten bigger and that old city is now the center of the widening circle. And now in those four quadrants, migrations have happened. Here's our map [Figure 1.2]. We have the four quadrants, but we've got Gillikin Heights and New Bunbury and all these other neighborhoods.

What happens if gentrification has happened in these different neighborhoods? So, the bottom layers of these cities, and the center of the city, is the old country. And it's growing out from there until stacks on stacks on stacks of different types of architecture showing different time periods are built upon each other [Figure 1.3]. In story and in design, we'll never throw anything away. We're always building upon what's been and that was a crucial central idea for us.

Mark Warshaw: Well, what's better than the foundation Baum laid out? It would be crazy to let that all go. Baum, in the later books, would just build upon what he'd already done – not being totally consistent. We could dig into all of his creations and pick and choose certain characters or certain story lines that served our needs.

Darin Mark: So, the character of General Guph becomes our big bad in the second season. Well, if you really try to get down at the brass tacks of history and how he still exists and where he's introduced in the canon and everything, it doesn't totally work. So, we're following our own Baumian logic as we're going on.

Mark Warshaw: We also took care in thinking of characters that could be immortal and could bridge those times. So, in our story, Glinda the Good is immortal. So, she was there and the Scarecrow

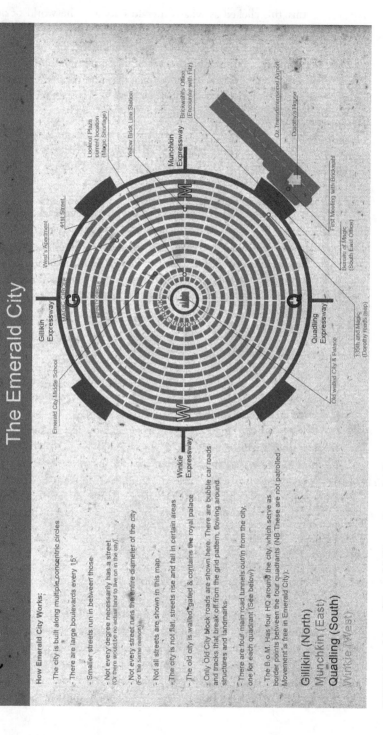

FIGURE 1.2 Map of Emerald City and surrounding environs

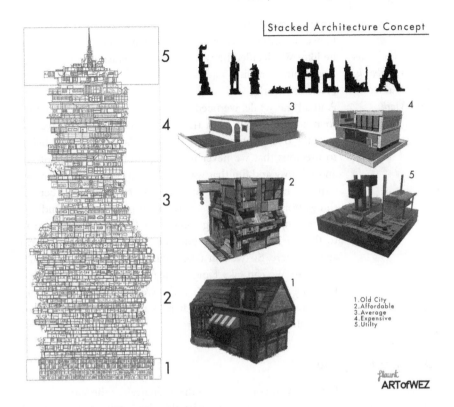

FIGURE 1.3 Stacked architecture concept

	too. So, they could serve as bridge characters coming from the Baum material to us.
Darin Mark:	In the original Baum books, there is so much negative capability; there were so many characters, places, and story lines running, some of which he never developed, some of which readers will not remember. One of our lead characters is Ojo, taken from Ojo the Unlucky, but we completely rebooted him. When we were deciding who we wanted to be regular characters on our series, we loved this guy. We saw a big opportunity in this character even though he didn't play a major role in the books. This character who felt unlucky because he had this curse on him triggered something within us. We keep exploring that character. We ended up redefining him completely. But those are springboards that we found throughout the books.

Mark Warshaw:	Another good example would be Reigh, our take on the Cowardly Lion. What would a contemporary Cowardly Lion be like? We decided he would be a conspiracy theorist . . .
Abram Makowka:	A conspiracy realist.
Mark Warshaw:	. . . in this world.
Jared Mark:	And all the while, we needed to allow ourselves the freedom to not be precious with the source material. While we are treating Baum's stories as the canon, there's a trap in being so precious that we never innovate and lose the spark of joy and whimsy and fun that was much a part of the IP. We always strive to honor the spirit of the books but also spoof certain things from our world in a way that is good-natured and fun but is actually also saying something. We wanted to be true to the spirit of the books but not limited to only what was already there. So we can take a character like Ojo and reinvent him. We can take King Roquat and completely redefine him as a child ruler in this world. We reimagined some core characteristics for modern audiences and, quite frankly, for our storytelling purposes.

Oz Is For Everyone

Henry Jenkins:	How do you conceptualize the audience for the show?
Mark Warshaw:	There was an edict to make this for a six- to 11-year-old demographic. But what we quickly realized is that Oz is for everybody. We saw their grandparents would watch *Oz*. They turned it on because it was something they recognized from their childhood, and they wanted to share Oz with their grandkids. We knew from, really, the get-go, that this is a story for everybody. And we didn't want to tell a story that was just for those kids. So, we definitely put the winks for people familiar with the source material. But also, we recognized that this was an opportunity to bring a brand-new world to most of the audience. Many children would be experiencing Oz for the first time through *Lost in Oz*. We were trying to encourage a co-viewing experience. We wanted *Lost in Oz* to be a show that everybody in the family could sit down and watch together.
Jared Mark:	So, we talked a lot about the shows that we watched growing up, the shows that we remember watching with our families. And I certainly have really special memories of laughing at sitcoms with my parents. Right now, there's such stratification of audiences and of screens. Every kid in the house might

have his or her own screen in his or her own hands. What kind of story today would get everybody watching one screen together? That was the real goal.

Abram Makowka: We were also fortunate not to come from children's TV. We all have told stories in other media that were for other age groups. And this is our first foray into the kids' space. So, we got to learn new ways to tell stories for kids and, at the same time, apply the bag of tricks we've gotten from working in other storytelling media.

Henry Jenkins: One of those bags of tricks, I guess, is seriality, which you deploy to a much greater degree than most children's television has done. What led to you creating *Lost in Oz* as a serial for kids?

Mark Warshaw: Well, the platform really dictates that. We were fortunate enough to be an early children's show in the streaming space. Streaming programs needed to be bingeable at that time. Here, because of the ways this content is distributed, we won't have to wait episodically.

They can sit down and watch this thing from start to finish. We wanted to make one big Pixar movie. We keep it serialized all the way through with that sophistication of storytelling. We really respect children and believe that they can handle a lot more than what they're usually given.

When we started building the show – it's been a little while now – at the time, *Game of Thrones* was hitting and *Breaking Bad*, and *The Wire* was a real touchpoint. All of these shows are not often discussed in terms of the creation of . . .

Henry Jenkins: I suspect if I was talking to *Tumbleleaf* producers,[4] they wouldn't be raising those.

Jared Mark: But for us, as fans of that kind of storytelling, we were all really thinking about what a family-friendly version of an epic serialized story would look like. You take this story, which at its core is centered around Dorothy and Toto, but very quickly, those relationships fall out, they get a lot of other characters involved and suddenly it becomes a really big cast, not unlike these big shows! We check in here, we check in there, these stories develop over time and over place and they sprawl in such a way that is really satisfying and really fun. We admired the way those stories weaved and came back and the different pairings of characters. We drew lessons from those series even as we built a family-friendly version.

We thought, "Well, that's something that can really separate this show. We can have an engaging story that unravels more like a book than episodic television". We call every episode a chapter for a reason. Our whole story started with the opening of the book and before that, it's based on books. We wanted children to have the experience of a novel opening up and expanding. Serial television is the closest thing we could offer.

Mark Warshaw: And of course, it was an Amazon show. They began as a book-store. They got the data that probably told them that they should do an Oz show, probably because they knew how many Oz books were being sold. So, this really beautiful perfect storm empowered us to tell our story like a novel.

Entering a World in Process

Henry Jenkins: So, what does that phrase "world-building" mean to you guys? How does world-building enter your creative process?

Mark Warshaw: World-building requires us to think through what kind of story world will provide the best opportunity to tell more of the story. We are sitting in the writer's room for the show here. The entire show is conceived basically at the table that you're sitting at right now. What elements can we put in that will inspire new stories? What happens when our characters bump up against those elements? What obstacles will they encounter as they move through this world? Dorothy is obviously a stranger in a strange land. What elements can we put into this world that will make it harder – or easier – for her to get home? The more you add to your world, the more exciting her story becomes. And then, on top of that, the visuals – the stunning nature of Oz – becomes the DNA of our story. How can you elevate these core elements of Oz to a whole other level?

And it really starts there. And then you start to get down to that granular nature of a world-build. We put Glinda as the head of the Bureau of Magic. The first person Dorothy meets is an officer from the Bureau of Magic, Agent Pugmill. And it is through these elements that you start to grow out your universe.

Abram Makowka: I think that's a good example of building out the logic of the world, so that when Dorothy is dropped into this place, it feels like she's dropped into a world that is already on its way. This just happens to be the first time we're getting a glimpse of it. So, there's a consistent logic that our audience starts to comprehend – this is the way things happen in Oz. What's the consistent tone of this world so that everything feels like it belongs? And then as soon as they feel like they have an understanding of that, we can turn it on its head.

Darin Mark: I was going to say, working off of that, how do you express the idea that a world is already up and running before your character enters into it? Throughout those early episodes, we have built in things that are old and shut down already: the subway station, which was itself a reinvention of the Yellow Brick Road, has been shuttered, and the main station is long gone. This deserted station on the Yellow Brick Subway Line will become the hideout for one of our evil characters, just another twist on it. All of this hints at some of the things that happened before our Dorothy ever arrived in Oz. When we step into this world, we step into the middle of the magic crisis. And we learn very quickly that magic is a commodity here. It's what fuels their society, its energy, its currency. When Dorothy enters the world, she discovers very quickly that there's a magic shortage. Nobody knows where it's going. There's some mystery already in play. People are already on the job trying to figure it out. How do you connect that to characters? Dorothy needs one of each of the magical elements in Oz in order to use magic to get home. So, the magic crisis plays directly into her story. We're not just tacking it on in the background. It actually connects to the character's main line.

The Periodic Table of Magical Elements

Jared Mark: Magic is a physical thing in this world. And so, we say, "What's the version of that in our world?" "The periodic table of elements". Everything in our world is made of atoms on the periodic table, and in this world, we have a periodic table of magic elements [Figure 1.4]. And so, we were able to create the chart literally classifying our world. But in terms of how to translate that visually, we put our periodic table not on a rectangular map, we put it on a circular chart. Everything in this world becomes circular.

We started saying, "What differentiates as we build this world? What differentiates Oz from Kansas, and color and shape become real keys to that". And our Kansas is an autumnal world of reds and oranges and yellows, square shapes, and angular lines. Whereas our Oz is greens and blues and yellows, but it's also a circular world with all of these bubble references; it's a circular environment.

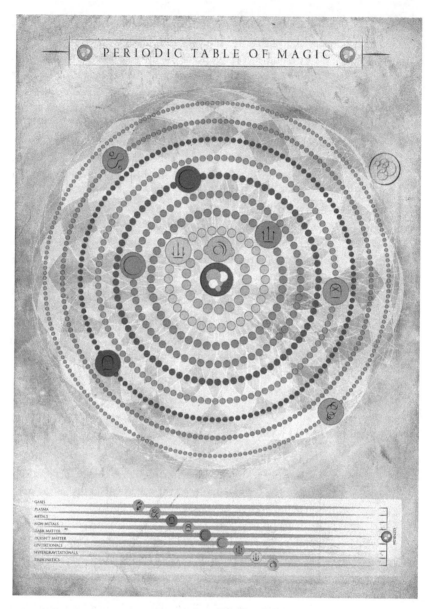

FIGURE 1.4   The Periodic Table of Magical Elements in Oz

Mark Warshaw: And then it also always goes back to how is this going to generate a good episode of television. So, if you have the periodic
table of magical elements and Dorothy has to collect one of
each of these hundred elements to get home, that also creates

a great driver for a particular episode because she's got to get a particular piece of magic to get home. That provides the opportunity for a 100 different episodes, really. We didn't use all of them but that did provide, at least, the DNA for potential plots of future episodes.

Henry Jenkins: So, how thoroughly did you work through the periodic table?

Jared Mark: Well, we go through it intentionally for our own storytelling needs. We broke it down in your basic classes: gases, plasmas, metals, nonmetals, dark matter, doesn't matter, levitational, hypergravitational, and telekinetic. And within those categories there are a number of elements.

So, when you see on screen as we zoom into this interactive periodic table, there might be a whole number of elements that we've never talked about within that. And so, as we built the series forward, we knew within those categories we need[ed] a magic that could break down the door. And so, we might say, "That would fit under a telekinetic type of magic". And within that, it might be X, Y, or Z. Now, we can name those as we go. People are still adding to our periodic table.

Mark Warshaw: Please understand that making television shows is such a collaborative process, and there's four creators of the show, but there's really 300 or 400 people that are creatively contributing to that show.

So, we need that room to grow the story out and add to the periodic table. We gave you the classifications, but we build on it across the stories because you never know where the best ideas are going to come from. Having the flexibility really helps when you're building out the series. We didn't have it so defined before day one. When you're laying out a world for a movie, you can nail it down a bit more. You have one story to tell and so you know what elements you will need to tell that story.

Creating these elements, these places, these sandboxes to play within, like the periodic table, where we have great boundaries in that sandbox, we have these classes of the different kinds of magic to work with, allows for just bountiful creativity. My wife is a great designer and when she designs, she loves to have one challenge in the design, one thing that she has to overcome to build a whole design around, something that tethers you down.

And having a couple of these places, these boundaries to work within, really helped to focus the creativity and makes it that much more rich.

Jared Mark: And this in turn influences our character design. We had this idea that, "Magic is physical. It's an actual thing and it's classified on this table". So, in this world, magic is science, and we have Dorothy who needs to get it to go home. We have a counterpart, West, who needs it because she is like a young, aspiring Olympic skater driven to be the best, except rather than ice skating, she's obsessed with magic. She's looking at it almost as an art form and her dream is to do things with magic that have never been done before. For her, magic involves a creative process. She's not a witch in the classic sense with evil machinations and just driven by power. She wants to be the best; she is extremely ambitious for the artistry of it. And so, suddenly, you've got this really interesting character built only because we have this idea of magic as a science.

And so, who is West's mother? That child's mother is Cyra, who is one of the greatest, most powerful witches that has ever been in all of the land. But long ago, she decided that the power game's not for her and she would rather be much more of a one-on-one magic specialist who is more of a healer and likened to a wellness physical therapist. And so, magic in this world has all of these different forms it can take. And so, for her, it's in this wellness shop whereas another character might use it to try to overtake the whole world. So, anyway, this one simple question – What are the elements that make up this world? – suddenly gives rise to all of the characters in our story.

Mark Warshaw: And allows us to be contemporary with that Cyra character. But then you go back through the books again. And you realize that magic as science was a thesis for Baum. In one of the books, Shaggy Man sings about science being magic in Oz and magic being science. Now, more than ever, we realize how science and magic get closer and closer to being the same thing in our more contemporary world – almost nothing feels impossible, probably, to our audience these days.

Abram Makowka: We ingested the canon and essentially set it to the side and said, "Now, we're going to create *Lost in Oz*". But the further we thought we got from Baum's creation, we'd then catch up on our research and realize, "There's a song for that. He did something just like that". So, it was almost like we opened ourselves up to the Baum matrix and as far as we tried to push it, there was always a tentacle of some things, so it all just started working together.

World-Sharing Practices

Henry Jenkins: How do we take a world that you four understand and translate it into a form that allows 300 people to work together to create the series? How does world-building become world-sharing?[5] What are some of the tools you use to communicate that world to other collaborators?

Mark Warshaw: It always starts with the script. The script in any medium — film, television — is the blueprint. So, the script had a lot of that, but we did a lot of briefs that helped everyone to learn what they needed to know about the world as we collaborated. A key part was collaborating with our art director in Scotland. His name's Stephen Donnelly. He was the first person that came back to us with the ideas that felt like he was taking the dreams we had and turned them into the visuals of the show. He really got the heart and soul of what we were going for and then built upon that. And so, he was a cocreator of what the world was going to be like. He really got the tenets that we were looking for. We made it clear that — these things we're talking about with you — this is the Emerald City that you read about in the books. But how have we aged it up now? Then you build visually on top of that. We went through a lot of iterations on what the look of this world would be like. But once you start to bring in supervising directors and other creatives around this stuff, they start to add to what the look and feel's going to be and it just grows and grows and grows. It was our job to keep it in the zone of our original vision but allow for that beautiful expansion of what things would look like.

Abram Makowka: This is our vision for the show, but every artist that joins us, they're going to bring something to it. So, how do we maintain that vision but also allow — and we always use this term — "the hand of the artist"? How do we allow that artist to take our vision and plus it? But plus it within that logic and tone of the world-building, so that our Oz remains consistent.

Henry Jenkins: When I talk to game designers, they often say the biggest challenge is figuring out what's not in the game. So, I'm wondering, given the expansiveness you're describing, how do you figure out what's not in the world or not parts of the world that we're going to see on screen? What are the limits?

Mark Warshaw: It's story.

Darin Mark: It's story. It's always story. We overdeveloped early on and had to very quickly understand that just because it's animation does not actually mean that "imagination is the limit". There is a barrier. Time and budget are the barriers and they're very real. So, we quickly learned that a lot of the things we had built into the scripts and we had our heart set on, we were going to have to choose seven out of the 20, no more. When it came to actual builds, we had to cut a lot of things. We learned quickly that we could do things like matte paintings for objects that characters aren't actually touching. This is getting a little technical here. But in digital animation, anything that is actually picked up, held, interacted with, has to be modeled and built into three-dimensional digital space, which comes with a price tag and a timetable. Once we knew we had to cut, let's say, 50 percent of the items that we created in our minds, you go back to [the] story right away. What's necessary to tell the story of this half-hour episode? Where's the camera pointing?

Abram Makowka: If the camera is only going to need three of four walls in a room, you don't build the fourth wall. And if Dorothy is just going to pass by a sign that was a wonderful Easter egg and we were all patting each other on the back because we just thought of something that's amazing, but it doesn't really change her trajectory through that story line – that's the thing that has to go.

Mark Warshaw: At the beginning. And once we actually had it all built out and knew what we would be working with in the end, we'd come in and add that stuff back in whenever we could. We'd rarely let something go on screen that didn't have a little bit of extra – I don't know, maybe an opportunity for a wink, opportunity to build out the world a little bit more. And so, we took those opportunities as much as we possibly could. We're not dealing with a major Pixar movie budget where you have hundreds of millions of dollars to play with it all. But the more detailed the world is, the more it just feels right – especially in a streaming place where you could go back and watch these things *over and over*. Kids repeat these episodes again and again, so if you wanted to dig beyond the surface, the details are there to bring the world to life.

And our background in transmedia led us to want to put in the details to ensure that there are other places to go in the fortunate case of being able to extend *Lost in Oz* to other platforms. So if you see a newspaper article on the screen, say, it is fully written out by our writing staff so we can extend into another medium when we are able to do so.

Darin Mark:	Because we are working in digital space, once an object is built, it can then be used as many times as you choose, and that allowed our world to grow with time. The accumulation of assets helps build out the story and you can notice it – giving away a little bit here – in some of the earlier episodes. There are really only about three or four characters that are in the backgrounds of these big city shots. They're just all wearing different colored clothes or hairstyles and slightly different sized, things like that, that don't actually change the geometric patterns of these characters. But as time goes on and we got to build more and more with each episode, the populations became very diverse and we ended up with lots of characters to fill our scenes. So, patience is important there.
Henry Jenkins:	And there's a sense that with each episode, we're opening up a little more of the world and I guess that reflects the same production process. The world gradually unfolds before us and each new story has opportunities for new pieces of the world. Baum himself talks about that in his intro to the various books, that "I'm now going to show you this corner of this world".
Mark Warshaw:	We thought of it as concentric circles. Starting in Emerald City and then expanding out to the Nome Kingdom across the desert, continuing out from there as Dorothy gets a little bit more comfortable in her surroundings and it becomes more of her home, showing a little bit more of that along the way.
Jared Mark:	It's like an expansive video game that you start and you're only allowed a portion of the map to explore, and as you get better, as you extend that story, then that world grows and grows.
Abram Makowka:	Again, we go somewhere because Dorothy needs to go there to figure something out, or Dorothy gets pulled there as a giant obstacle in the way of her achieving her goal.
Jared Mark:	In that first episode, Dorothy's first success in this new world is finding her way from Point A to Point B on a map and then when she gets there, it's closed. There's an immediate roadblock.

But we talked a lot about how to make that experience relatable for a kid viewer. It's their first day in a new school, finding your class, first day in a new city when your family moves, first day in a new country if you're an immigrant. Often the first success is figuring out how to navigate your surroundings. |

The Map

Henry Jenkins:	So, the map is literally an important part of the design process but also figures in a lot of the plots in the story. We can take that all the way back to Baum doing those original maps that often appeared in the front or back of the books. I see that you've got Baum's original maps on the wall of the studio.
Jared Mark:	And it even becomes a real fun Easter egg: we have a magic map deep in season two.
Mark Warshaw:	Those maps also are a necessary piece of the puzzle when you're producing the show because the directors often end up asking, "What does it look like outside of West's bedroom? What direction is she looking? When she looks in that direction, what's there?" You really need to map that stuff out to communicate across to all the scenes. So, when you asked earlier on, what are some of the tools we used, mapping the world was one of the earliest steps we took. We said, "We're just going to stop here", and build a map of the world. So, everybody knows which direction West faces when she's looking out her bedroom window, where is that Yellow Brick Line, where does the Bureau of Magic reside. And that's such a helpful tool that helps to generate moves in stories too.
Abram Makowka:	And back to the logic of the world-building, as soon as you put it on a map, it's real; it exists. You can look down on it and say, "Where is Dorothy within the context of where she was?" And everybody can now look at this and say, "What we're doing is real. It exists". To your question before about, how do you contain it all, well, now, it's on a map; we can anchor it.
Mark Warshaw:	Maps are exceptional storytelling tools. The spatial relationship between your characters and the places that they visit within the world help you block out their moves. And when you get to the point where you're working with your storyboarding teams and they need to know where Dorothy's running to in this particular scene, that stuff just really helps out a lot.
Jared Mark:	And it's so fun to do and this gets into the question you had before about instilling our vision and ensuring that our vision should translate to all the artists involved. Stephen Donnelly did such a great job with this. So, in the pilot episode, we wrote that Dorothy needs to find her way to 41st Street and Infinity. That was the cross street. We thought that was a fun idea. Then we started getting into the world design and talking about what this map actually looks like. We were playing with

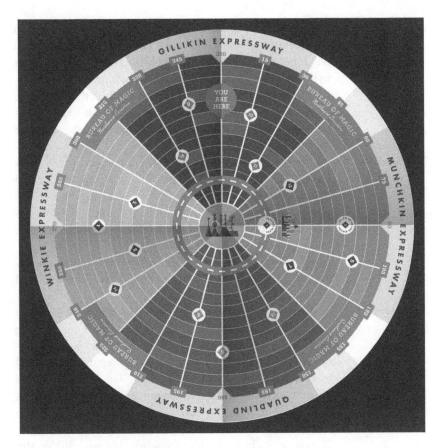

FIGURE 1.5   Circular map of Oz

a circular map [Figure 1.5]. Suddenly Stephen Donnelley had a brilliant idea: "There are 360 degrees in a circle, so there are 360 Streets – 1st Street all the way around until 360th Street and West is on 41st Street. That immediately puts her in this quadrant and Infinity Circle is one of those surrounding streets". And suddenly, what was just one tossed off gag in the pilot script starts to set the coordinates of the world and gradually helps us map every other event in the series.

Dorothy's Journal

Henry Jenkins: And the other tool, I guess, is Dorothy's journal, which plays important functions in the world-building here as well. Could you say a little bit about what the role the journal is playing for you?

Abram Makowka: The journal connects us to the history. It contains information about all that has happened, what Dorothy will come to find out. It makes that backstory tangible. And then it also connects to the idea that science is magic. She's holding a tangible magical book in her hand that has a technology to it, that has a logic to it. It asks her questions, it tells her, "Go forth". She doesn't know the rules, but that book is full of rules that she's going to have to catch up on.

Jared Mark: And it was from Oz. So, it's a link to the canon for us. It's a link to a lineage that she doesn't know anything about and that she'll learn about over time. And it's a magic book – its images can populate over time, which very much like the periodic table is really helpful for storytelling purposes, for asset-building, for all of that stuff.

We build what we need as it goes, but for Dorothy, knowledge of this world and her history unveils over time as needed for story.

Mark Warshaw: And it's also a fun way to illustrate the evolution of Oz, from the Dorothy people might know from the books to the Dorothy we're sending to Oz, because this magical tornado, now, could literally be replicated and generated on demand by opening up this journal and saying, "Go forth". And then when she actually gets to Oz and immediately butts up against Pugmill, Dorothy learns that this is a different era than this journal came from. Magic used to be easy to come by just 20 years ago when your mom was here, but you can't do this today because Oz is in the middle of a magic crisis so you're stuck here in Oz. The journal became a prop to help generate that part of that story.

Dorothy the Engineer

Henry Jenkins: I'm always intrigued by the game-like mechanisms that are woven into the world of Oz, which seems to go hand-in-hand with Dorothy as a puzzle solver, as an engineer. So, could you talk about what you borrow from games as you think about the world? Is that conscious or . . .

Darin Mark: I don't know if it's conscious. I don't think any of us are heavy-duty gamers.

Mark Warshaw: Well, Dorothy being a puzzle solver and also someone who is really mechanical, that did influence the world quite a bit. So, there are gears all over Oz and machinations of how things are fit together. Right from the very get-go, she has the Rube

Goldberg machine in her home back in Kansas and we place similar elements in Oz so that she could then take things apart and put them together to solve puzzles to get out of jams.

Jared Mark: We always say that Dorothy's greatest strength and her greatest weakness are the same thing: she cannot let a problem go unsolved. That is who she is at her core. And so, that's a very game-like idea and to her, any problem immediately becomes a puzzle to solve. We go into Dorothy's vision every once in a while, where she's stuck in a predicament, hanging from a rope, and she looks around her and at the tools at hand. We want our viewers to figure out how she is going to solve this urgent problem with just the MacGyver-style tools at hand. That's certainly game logic – what is my inventory, what is the problem, how do I go about this insurmountable challenge with a great attitude and sense of fun? That's a game right there no matter what.

Mark Warshaw: What's "play" and what's "fun"? Like running through the night market and how those are hovering kiosks and you would jump from level to level and rise up or drop down. Games definitely influenced the set design of those environments.

Henry Jenkins: Well outside the Nome Palace, there is Crush Canyon, and to solve it, the characters have to count out the rhythm of the mechanism. And that's classic Super Mario Brothers stuff. That's the sort of thing that I'm thinking about that seems to be an acknowledgment of a video-game-raised generation of kids.

Abram Makowka: Well, I think that that's what it is. I think that it's embedded in us. It's in the way that we treat our villains. Like in the classic video games that we grew up on, you came up against the first bad guy. And once you defeated him, you leveled up to the next bad guy. But we didn't consciously pull it from the games we grew up on, we pulled that from the shows that we're referencing.

Mark Warshaw: For us, that is like *Breaking Bad* or *The Wire*. Your challenges are born out of the characters that you have to work with. So, you've got Dorothy, she's a puzzle solver; you got Crush Canyon that came from Baum, we just updated it, and that's a great puzzle for her to solve. She's got to discover that there's a rhythm and work within the rhythm to cross to the other side basically. As much as we're maybe not gamers now, we definitely all had our Nintendo games growing up.

Jared Mark: By the time Crush Canyon comes into our story, we've already spent the first half of that season collaborating with our sound designers who are amazing. And so, we were thinking of what's a fun challenge that we're going to come up against. And for the first time in our show, we created an audio puzzle to solve. Really, it becomes a rhythmic sound puzzle which is really fun. Again, enlisting the brilliance of our collaborators to really help with that.

Darin Mark: Our Dorothy is not a nonmagical being. She's an engineer in a world of magic. So, she looks at magical systems from an engineering point of view. So, early in the series, Dorothy is in the night market and Fitz is throwing these water balloons that are going to erase her memory. Dorothy has already discovered that there are these magical portals that she can jump through. They're sold at a flea market and she starts using them as a game. Instead of getting blasted by these memory-erasing water balloons, she dives into a portal and shoots out on the other side. And she starts taunting the villain to try to hit her and she's ducking in and out of these portals. She's not magical, but she's using it in order to get out of this situation.

Reading the Concept Art

Mark Warshaw: One of the fun challenges we had was how do you make a thrilling adventure with very little violence? And what are the challenges you can put your characters up against that aren't the traditional superhero, "I should defeat the supervillain with my fist or with a laser gun" route. And I think that definitely contributed to the way we built this conflict around water balloons and escape portals.

We thought from the start that Emerald City should almost feel like a giant amusement park. And so, we have the Ferris wheels and the massive set pieces in the very first episode. Being on a streamer, we know that people look at the first frame and decide if they actually want to go into this world and see that show.

And so, if you look at some of our key art, that's the idea behind all of that stuff, those colors and the fun of a Ferris wheel, the little girl on the back of a flying monkey, that kind of stuff is meant to be fulfilling and fun. We wanted to create a space where you want to go travel to after school or with your family on a holiday weekend.

So, these are the two pieces that Amazon commissioned during the green-lighting process [Figure 1.6]. And as much as it was about getting the character right because she wasn't

FIGURE 1.6 The concept art that helped the series get accepted at Amazon

        totally right yet, and you can see they're in the early stages of these guys, so much time was spent on the world here, putting those gears in, creating that stacked architecture that you may recognize as inspired by the flavelas in Rio. The clustered living and mismatched structures all bundled together form something unique and beautiful. And that is the top of the Yellow Brick Line in there. This was a highly analyzed piece of artwork: we spent a very tense yet exciting hour of our lives walking through what felt like almost every pixel of this picture with the head of the studio. And this is the ultimate piece of art that he said, "You guys are green-lit, go make a pilot that looks like that".

Jared Mark:	There are so many details that we've already thought out at this time …
Mark Warshaw:	The Lookout's fingers?
Jared Mark:	Yes. And she's climbing on the Lookout's fingers. He's an actual magical being who was turned to stone long enough ago that he's got moss and stuff growing on his hands.
Jared Mark:	So, this image [Figure 1.7] conveys the whimsy and fun of our hero kids and a cute dog and the adventure they're on while also referencing *Blade Runner*.
Abram Makowka:	*Blade Runner* for kids.
Jared Mark:	This concept art became a frame of the show.
Darin Mark:	It never changed, never changed.
Jared Mark:	It's everything in one image!
Mark Warshaw:	When we saw this, we saw the show. We knew what the show looked like. And if you look, here we have an airport in Oz,

FIGURE 1.7 Concept art of the Emerald City downtown, inspired by *Blade Runner* (1982)

it's literally on the same spot that Dorothy landed on in the original book [Figure 1.8]. That was the idea – there's sort of this portal system, this landing spot for tornadoes carrying houses from other dimensions. And they built an airport on top of it because they had studied this area to find out how to do inter-dimensional travel when there was enough magic to do so. And our Dorothy shows up and she finds a shuttered airport. Everything's grounded at this airport at this time.

Jared Mark: Because there's no magic left to run all the planes and blimps and flying machines.

Henry Jenkins: So, talk about Dorothy's house there. It's a very different style obviously than MGM imagined or than in the Baum books, so what went into that design choice?

Jared Mark: We wanted to avoid the pastoral version of Oz. It felt familiar. And so, our version of Dorothy's house is a modernization of what came before. In Kansas, she lives in a suburban neighborhood, not a farm neighborhood and . . .

Abram Makowka: So, we gave her a mid-century modern home. Another version of bridging between the books and the time that we're in now that feels timeless.

Jared Mark: Ojo says, "Not a lot of mid-century modern ranch houses in Oz".

Abram Makowka: But that's also a popular throwback style of house today. So, what it says is about Dorothy and Evelyn – they're cool, they've got a style to them.

FIGURE 1.8   Concept art for the Oz airport

Mark Warshaw:	It's familiar but fresh, the way people update those houses.
Jared Mark:	Her house is angular, rectangular, and triangular in a very circular world that she just landed in. And you get the autumnal colors of her house and her sweater, looking at this very gold, blue, and green world.
	All these flying machines and flying – they're circular – there's a circular runway and a cylindrical airport terminal building and balloon-like structures. And so, here she is, this is the moment. We've really thought a lot about how beautifully well done the MGM film was as everything went from black and white to color when she landed in Oz. We knew that we couldn't do that; that movie is very well protected. We needed our own version of something visual as we go from Dorothy's world to Oz. And this is the moment, this is literally the moment she opens her door and sees this new world for the first time. And so, a lot of thought went into what that first crack at the door is going to reveal.
Henry Jenkins:	Can you help me understand the role which concept art plays in the production process?
Mark Warshaw:	So, concept art works before you move into the direction of finalizing what the architectural plans will be for building out your environments and building your characters. It also helps you get the tone down from a lighting perspective.

So, you really feel that piece of concept art. You feel the story there; you feel the majesty that we're looking for. The concept art helps everyone involved in the decision-making process to feel the story that you're trying to tell. So, it is a fantastic communication tool. After you have your script, or at least your strong concept, in a written form, an artist will take it and create a piece of art to really rally the teams around it and give them something to work off of.

Jared Mark: It's a really good communication tool to ensure that we're on the same page. We knew right away that Ojo is a giant Munchkin. We want our Dorothy to be a girl who doesn't – maybe has skinned knees or doesn't mind getting dirty – she's action oriented, so we need her to be able to move and so we know we need her in some kind of clothes that wouldn't be too stiff. We had all these different ideas. These characters are very different from the way these characters ended up, but you start to see the DNA that leads us from this Dorothy to this one. As we start to work with these designs, our director gives us choices that help us refine the characters: "We are working with these different types of hair, which one feels better to you?" And these discussions go back and forth until together we land on something where everyone sees the same thing.

Abram Makowka: It's all words and ideas to begin with and we just start trying things. It's the research and development period.

Jared Mark: There are four of us at the table with, I would say, really different personal tastes and preferences. I don't think this show would look anything close to what it looks like if only one of us were creating it. It really, truly is a collaborative art form that would not exist the way it does without all the different cooks in that kitchen.

Notes

1. See, for example, Henry Jenkins, "'All Over the Map': Building (and Rebuilding) Oz", in Mark J. P. Wolf, editor, *Revisiting Imaginary Worlds: A Subcreation Studies Anthology*, New York: Routledge, 2017, pp. 172–191; Micheal O. Reilly, *Oz and Beyond: The Fantasy World of L. Frank Baum*, Lawrence, Kansas: University Press of Kansas, 1992; Frank Kelleter, "'Toto, I Don't Think We Are in Kansas Again and Again and Again: Remakes and Popular Seriality", in Kathleen Loock and Constantine Vervis, editors, *Film Remakes, Adaptations and Fan Productions*, New York: Palgrave Macmillan, 2012, pp. 19–44.
2. For more on Baum as a prototypical transmedia creator, see Matthew Freeman, *Historicizing Transmedia Storytelling: Early Twentieth-Century Transmedia Story Worlds*, London: Routledge, 2016.

3. Geoffrey Long, "Creating Worlds in Which to Play: Using Transmedia Aesthetics to Grow Stories into Storyworlds", in Benjamin W. I. Derhey Kurtz and Melanie Bourdaa, editors, *The Rise of Transtexts: Challenges and Opportunities*, London: Routledge, 2016, pp. 139–152.
4. *Tumnbleleaf* is another series – for preschoolers – which is produced for Amazon.
5. I draw the concept of world-sharing from Derek Johnson, *Media Franchising: Creative License and Collaborating in the Culture Industries*, New York: New York University Press, 2013.

2

THE MAKING OF *MUD*

Three Stories of Genesis

Richard A. Bartle

What Was *MUD*?

MUD was the progenitor of today's massively multiplayer online role-playing games (MMORPGs for short, MMOs for shorter). Pretty much every present-day MMO is a direct descendent of *MUD* in the sense of its being a virtual world.

The game was created in October 1978, so reached its 40th anniversary in 2018. It's still playable (and indeed played) today, but time has moved on; it was written in the days of punched cards, teletypes, and text, but modern games are graphical (hence, *video* games). As a consequence, *MUD* is mainly remembered for what it was, rather than for what it is.

Virtual worlds are first and foremost worlds. In the same way that different cultures in our world have origin stories, so do different virtual worlds. *TinyMUD* (1989), for example, came about as a reaction to the excessive use of combat in *AberMUD* (1987). *DikuMUD* (1991) came about in response to the freedom to concentrate on gameplay after the people who preferred socializing left for *Tiny-MUD*. *EverQuest* (1999) came about because its designers wanted to recreate the *DikuMUD* experience employing graphics instead of text.

MUD is no different from other virtual worlds with regard to its having a backstory. Its origins are, however, perhaps more noteworthy because nothing came before it. The genesis of *World of Warcraft* (2004) is complex but defers at least in part to *EverQuest*; the same applies to *EverQuest*, which defers to *DikuMUD*; *DikuMUD*'s beginnings are similarly rich and relate strongly to *Dungeons & Dragons* (1974), but in its virtual worldliness, the game defers directly to *AberMUD*, which in turn defers to *MUD*. *MUD* doesn't defer to anything, because this is where the genealogy stops. Whence, then, did it come?

I was one of the two people who brought *MUD* into being. When asked about the game's origins, the answer I give depends on who is asking the question and why. There are three main reasons people want to know about *MUD*'s origins, for which I have three corresponding responses. Each of these mythologizes the game's genesis, favoring a different worldview. I've used all of them stand-alone many times in past conversations and presentations and continue to do so. All that's changed over the years is the relative number of times I've given each answer, which has altered as more and more people have come to think about how games are made, what language they use to speak to their players, and what they are being used to say.

Initially, I gave a craft-oriented account, describing *MUD* in terms of the events related to its programming. Later, when I was asked about it by people who were designing their own virtual worlds, I gave a design-oriented account, explaining how the various mechanics interacted with one another and what they were intended to mean. It was perhaps a quarter of a century after work on *MUD* began that I was able to give a third, art-oriented, account that stood a fighting chance of being what a conference audience wanted to hear.

In this essay, I shall present these three accounts. From them, the reader is invited to divine their own composite account of the origins of *MUD* in particular and therefore of virtual worlds in general.

As Craft

In common with most university computer science departments in the late 1970s, the one at Essex University in the UK had a hacker culture.

This culture was, as elsewhere, emergent. The combination of logical thinking and creative expression required of programmers back then drew to the subject people who had a certain core set of attitudes and abilities. It wasn't that an individual arrived at a computer science department and was inculcated into its belief systems; rather, it was that that to be interested in, and able to program, computers in those days, a person had to look at the world a certain way. When they arrived at university, they were pleasantly surprised to find that the other people studying the subject shared that same perspective. Computers were devices for freedom and fun, intrinsically interesting because of what they were, but also useful as tools to do who-knows-what with for the benefit of humanity. Computers were all potential, and it was taken for granted that everyone working with them wished to explore that potential because, well, why wouldn't they?

One day (probably the Friday) in the week beginning Monday, October 16, 1978, a group of perhaps half a dozen computer science undergraduates at Essex University were sitting around in the room where the computer terminals were, reading manuals. This was normal, because for these students, reading manuals was a joyful and communal activity; if you saw something interesting, you'd mention it, and the others present would chip in with comments and ideas of what could be done with it or how what it was intended to achieve could be done better some other way.

On this particular day, one of these students, Roy Trubshaw, was looking for ideas on how to get around a problem he had. He'd hoped to use some system calls relating to inter-process communication (IPC), which would allow one program to talk to another program without going through shared files (which were slow and messy to use). Unfortunately, regular programmers weren't allowed to use IPC because message packets were a limited resource. One mistake could mean that not only did the student's program fail to work but that the whole operating system would also seize up. The university's computer was a DECsystem-10 mainframe, used under time-sharing: if all the IPC packets were tied up accidentally (or deliberately) by a single program, no one in the whole university could use the DEC-10 until it had been switched off and the lengthy process of rebooting completed. Bye-bye all the work you'd been doing if that happened.

In one of the manuals, Roy came across a system call named SETUWP.

SETUWP allowed the user to set the write protection of a memory segment. The architecture of the DEC-10 was such that memory was divided into two segments when looked at from the point of view of a user. The high segment contained code and was shareable. The low segment contained data and was non-shareable. The rationale behind this sharing regime was that if 40 students (say) were all using the same text editor at once, there would only need to be one copy of the code in memory (because all students would be running the same program) but there would need to be 40 different sets of data (because each student would be editing a different file). The rationale behind the protection regime was that changing shared code was problematic (because a change for one user would be a change for all), and changing unshared data was unproblematic (because any changes made wouldn't affect everyone else).

Put simply, then, the high segment was shared for efficiency reasons and write-protected for security reasons.

SETUWP would allow Roy to make the high segment writeable.

He brought his discovery to the attention of the other students, and they agreed that what he wanted to do sounded feasible. He'd write an assembly-language program consisting of code (which he didn't want to overwrite) followed by a whole bunch of zeroes (which he did want to overwrite). He'd use the space occupied by those zeroes as a place to put data. If two users were running the same program, then whatever he overwrote the zeroes with would be visible to both. If one instance of the program put a message in there, the other instance of the program would see it when it checked and could display it to its user.

Roy immediately went to a teletype and wrote a technology test. It took him about two hours, because he had to be extremely careful. Accidentally overwriting code with data would cause a crash when any attempt to execute it was made; accidentally overwriting code with code would cause a crash if any user was executing that code while it was being changed. He had to make sure he only overwrote the zeroes, not the code, and that he didn't do so when another user was reading from or writing to that piece of memory. Amazingly, this rather complicated program – which replicated much of what IPC could do – worked the first time.

Roy labeled his project *MUD*, an acronym for its full name: *Multi-User Dungeon*. He had big plans for it.

Immediately, he discarded this first version and began work on version 2. Also written in assembly language, he had it fully working by mid-December; it would easily be recognizable to today's players as a simple but nevertheless fully fledged virtual world.

I became involved shortly after Roy had begun work on this version 2 of *MUD*. I had started at university only a few weeks earlier, whereas Roy was in his second year (of three); we initially hooked up when I joined the Computer Society, of which Roy was secretary.

I was very interested in games and had some experience of designing them, so I began to create what would now be called "content" for *MUD*. Content is what players consume when they play: it includes locations, creatures, objects, and things to do. Roy still created most of it, and one or two other members of the Computer Society apart from me also chipped in. The code remained all Roy's.

This second version of *MUD* was expanded over the course of the next year with additional functionality and content. It became apparent, however, that the program was beginning to become unwieldy. Programmer speed is measured in fully debugged lines per day, which tends to remain constant whatever program-ming language is used; Roy is an exceptionally fast programmer, but assembly language is less expressive than a high-level language, so it takes more lines to say the same thing. Also, the code to add new content to *MUD* was built into the game itself, taking up memory that could have been used for the content itself or for additional functionality. Worse, all new content was stored in the program executable binary, not as a separate data file; this meant that whenever the program was reassembled to add new functionality or to fix bugs, all the content, added since the last time an executable file was created, disappeared. The only content left would be the parts Roy had hard-coded in.

Roy realized that this was not the best way to go about things, so he was determined to write a command to dump content from memory so it could be read back in when the game was restarted after a patch. This worked, but it stored everything – preserving players and messages as well as content changes. He could have cleaned the data block up before dumping it, but this looked to be a tremendous amount of work. He snapped and decided instead to rewrite the entire game from scratch as version 3. Instead of assembly language, he would use the high-level systems programming language BCPL, which was standard at the time at Essex University. A beautiful language, it's the parent of the parent of C;

importantly for Roy's reliance on SETUWP, BCPL interfaced seamlessly with MACRO-10, the DEC-10's assembly language.

In this rewrite, Roy removed the content-creation part of the game to an off-line program he called DBASE. He created a *MUD* definition language (MUDDL) that was used to define the virtual world; DBASE took the MUDDL world description, compiled it into a memory dump file, which *MUD* itself would then read in and bake into the executable. This allowed content to be created piecemeal while *MUD* was running and for it to be better curated. In version 2, which allowed players to create content during play, the results were often substandard: they were badly spelled, with poor grammar and punctuation, and they were frequently inconsistent, contradictory, incomplete, or incoherent. Switching to MUDDL, new content could be checked and edited very easily, and its quality and house style maintained.

Roy's work on *MUD* version 3 progressed rapidly, but at the cost of his academic work. He had a final-year project to write and around Easter 1980 accepted that he probably ought in fact write it if he wanted a degree. He'd produced around a quarter of the code for *MUD* version 3 at this point (the most important quarter). So as to concentrate on his academic studies, he handed over code ownership (that is, final editorial control) to me. Being a year younger than Roy, my finals weren't to loom until 1981, so over the summer I finished off the *MUD* engine and wrote almost all its content.

By now, people outside the university environment were playing the game. Version 2 had been played from a handful of other universities over what would later become the Internet, courtesy of Essex University's proximity to the post office telecommunications research campus at Martlesham Heath. Version 3 was additionally played by people from home if they had a modem and could afford the UK's very steep long-distance telephone charges. So many of them came that the university restricted login times to a midnight-to-6:00 a.m. window on weekdays, but the game was nevertheless always full. People would connect an hour before they would be allowed to play, simply to ensure they had a line when the time came. Eventually, several of these players clubbed together and bought the university more modems so that more of them had overnight access to the game.

It's hard today to appreciate what the experience of playing *MUD* was like back then. Today's MMO players have cut their teeth on many games beforehand, but for many *MUD* players, *MUD* was their first computer game of any kind. Playing in a world that was of reality but was not reality was an utterly awesome experience. Were you to log in to *MUD* today, you may be impressed by its depth and detail, but you wouldn't be anywhere near as impressed by the very concept itself because it's now old hat. For its first players, however, *MUD* was literally a new world.

Unsurprisingly, some of the people who played *MUD* were inspired to create their own virtual worlds. This, they did, and in time, this type of game came to be known as a MUD. To disambiguate it from the genre that bore its name, *MUD* itself was subsequently referred to as *MUD1* by players, most of whom weren't aware that it was actually the third version of the game. The name stuck.

Roy and I encouraged people to write their own MUDs. After I completed my BSc, I stayed on at Essex University to do a PhD in artificial intelligence (so I could make the mobiles – the computer-controlled denizens of *MUD* – behave more intelligently); in my spare time, I continued to improve and expand *MUD1*. Eventually, I too snapped, and rewrote it all over again as version 4, which, of course, wound up being called *MUD2*. This is the current version of the game.

The process of dissemination had already begun though. People played *MUD*, liked the idea, and wrote their own MUDs. Some of these were good, some were bad. Players were inspired by them to write their own MUDs, and so the family tree began. *AberMUD* was one such game, which in its own fourth version was ported to Unix; its author, Alan Cox, later went on to become a major figure in the development of Linux. *AberMUD* was introduced to the United States by Michael Lawrie, who administrated many of the MUDs running on UK university computers at the time.

Once the United States picked up the game, the popularity of MUDs increased tremendously. Many US universities used Unix, and telephone charges were much lower in North America than in Europe. As a result, MUDs there were far more accessible than in Britain. At their peak, just before the launch of the World Wide Web, MUDs accounted for around 11 percent of all the bits on the main Internet backbone.

It's important to note that *MUD* does not represent the only occasion that virtual worlds were invented. At least five others sprang independently from the minds of their designers: *Avatar* (1979) by Bruce Maggs, Andrew Shapira, and David Sides; *Sceptre of Goth* (1978) by Alan Klietz; *Island of Kesmai* (1985) by Kelton Flinn and John Taylor; *Habitat* (1985) by Randy Farmer and Chip Morningstar; and *Monster* (1986) by Rich Skrenta. Why, then, are today's virtual worlds almost exclusively descendants of *MUD* rather than any of the others (all of which originated in the United States)?

The answer is that none of the others particularly encouraged their players to write their own games based on them. *Monster* is a possible exception, but it appeared over a decade after *MUD* so didn't have as long to build up momentum. Roy and I did encourage people to create MUDs of their own, and this attitude was in turn promulgated by those who were so encouraged. The other developers tended to guard their code (in the cases of *Sceptre of Goth*, *Island of Kesmai*, and *Habitat* for perfectly understandable commercial reasons), but the *MUD* ethos was to be open to anyone interested in making their own virtual world. *Avatar* came from a similar hacker culture to *MUD*, so it can reasonably be expected to have shared a similar enthusiasm for spreading its word, but sadly it only ran on the PLATO network – effectively a walled garden from which escape into the wider world was difficult.

Roy and I felt that because development of the game had ultimately been funded by the largesse of the British taxpayer through the medium of our student grants, we ourselves had no right to ownership of the concept of a MUD. Besides, the somewhat draconian terms of use of Essex University's Computing Service were such that anything developed on the DEC-10 in theory actually belonged to the university, not to the programmers. I approached the university with a view to its relinquishing this ownership in the case of *MUD* and met with a positive response: the university actively wished to disassociate itself from something as potentially bad for publicity as a computer game – especially one played by people over whom it had no influence, who might do all manner of disreputable things. This was rather far-sighted of it, as matters turned out. So it was that in 1985 I was able to put the concept of virtual worlds into the public domain, thereby ensuring that anyone who did write (or had already written) their own need not fear that we or the university might sue them over it.

The result of this culture of free dissemination meant that by the mid-1990s virtual worlds descended from *MUD* outnumbered those from other sources thousands to one. When commercial companies became interested in making virtual worlds, they naturally looked to the amateur ones to recruit their staff. The preponderance of *MUD*-heritage developers meant that many, many more of them were available to found the MMORPG industry, and so the graphical worlds we have today draw almost exclusively on *MUD* origins when it comes to their multiplayer gameplay and the sense of what it is to *be* a virtual world.

I say "almost exclusively" because a few players of *Sceptre of Goth* were inspired by it to write their own games. Some of those games were successful and inspired others, so forming a tributary that later joined the *MUD* river. It's therefore fair to say that some modern MMORPGs (in particular *Dark Age of Camelot* (2001) and the forthcoming *Camelot Unchained*) can ultimately trace their lineage back to *Sceptre of Goth* rather than to *MUD*.

So concludes this summary of the origins of *MUD*, mythologized in terms of the craft that went into its creation. The finding of an obscure system call, a small prototype, the creation of a world, two further rewrites, a belief in open software, a little evangelizing, some insularity on the part of competition: so it is that virtual worlds began.

To the best of my recollection, all this is correct.

It's historically correct, in terms of its description of the events that happened and the order in which they happened. It's causally correct, in that each event described led to what is claimed to be a consequence.

It doesn't describe *MUD*'s origins at all.

As Design

1978 was a wondrous, exciting time to be making a world.

Computers were laughably weak, computer games were novelties, the main user interface was text, there was no Internet, and fantasy was still establishing itself as a bona fide literary genre.

This meant everything was being done for the first time. It was bliss.

As it happened, I had made worlds before.

Some six years earlier, when I was 12, I'd bought from the local newsagent one of the 135 × 170 mm letter-writing pads that were my only reliable and affordable source of paper. I often used them to make games and on this occasion was planning to create something different. I took out all the sheets and stuck them together with sticky tape to form a large snaking whole that covered much of the floor in our front room. I then turned it over (because felt tips won't write on sticky tape) and drew a map.

As I drew, I was imagining an undiscovered continent. I knew some basic geography from school, so I had mountains in chains and rivers running from high ground to the sea, and I kept deserts away from jungles. I didn't know how plate tectonics worked, however, so the placing of the mountains didn't entirely make sense in retrospect. Also, the jungles turned into regular forest when my dark-green felt-tip pen ran out.

I populated this unexplored continent with natural wonders and native villages. Some such villages were in hidden valleys, some were parts of extensive kingdoms, and some were on the coast and so were aware of the wider world. Some were at war or were suffering from proximity to mosquito-infested swamps or were at risk from mudslides.

I took two pins and taped them together like dividers, with a fixed width of 30 mm between their points. One millimeter represented one mile (I wasn't bothered about mixing units). In the absence of anything in the local library to tell me otherwise, this was how far I figured a person could walk in a day.

Into this world, I introduced an explorer: Dr Toddystone. The time period was that of the age of imperialism, and Dr Toddystone was an intrepid explorer trying to be the first to get from one side of the continent to the other. He started at one of the friendly ports, where he bought provisions and hired some guards and bearers; then he set off at a rate of 30 miles a day into uncharted territory. I marked his progress on the map with a freehand black line. I recorded what he did each day in the form of a diary, written as if by Dr Toddystone himself.

Sometimes, Dr Toddystone would do what I wanted and, say, head for the mountain where I knew there was a spectacular waterfall he could name after himself. Other times, he would get himself into some annoying fix that would have followed as a consequence of his earlier actions, which meant he couldn't find the ruins of an ancient city or the plant that could cure influenza. If he hadn't gone into that gold mine, the natives wouldn't be after him, and he wouldn't have lost two bearers and a donkey crossing a river in a hurry, so he'd have to follow the river south looking for another village rather than head west toward where vast herds of animals roamed.

So, what had I done here?

Well, I'd created a world entirely in my imagination and then visited that world through the vehicle of Dr Toddystone. Only *I* could visit the world, because only I could be Dr Toddystone.

When I read back the diaries afterward, the words were dead on the page. That wasn't the point though: the fun came from writing them in the first place, to turn what was previously a vaguely defined haze of possibilities into a concrete series of events.

I was using (what I thought of as) a game as a machine to create stories.

Dr Toddystone went on seven adventures across three continents over the summers of 1972–1974. I threw out the maps and the diaries when I was done with them; all that remained of the game were my own memories and experience of designing and playing it.

I read *The Lord of the Rings* (1954–1955) three times in my teens (I think Roy Trubshaw read it even more). This wasn't because the story was particularly good – it was pretty bad, in fact. It wasn't even because of the world that Tolkien had built, because although I really liked it in parts, there were other components that just didn't hang together. In particular, the mountains surrounding Mordor were a joke even to someone with my limited understanding of how continents formed.

No, the reason I read, reread, and re-reread the book was because it was a proof of concept. It showed that it was possible to create a (largely) believable imaginary world and then to visit it as if it were real, treating it absolutely straight – as fact, rather than fiction. It showed to me that it was practical to realize an obviously made-up world in such detail that it seemed no less real to the reader than anywhere else they'd never been to but had heard existed.

When I first read about *Dungeons & Dragons*, I immediately grokked the concept. I knew from having played *Dr Toddystone* what role-playing was and so understood exactly what *D&D* would entail. In the two years prior to going to university, I spent many of my leisure hours playing the game. Because several of us had clubbed together to buy the rule books, we took it in turns to be dungeon masters. I waited patiently and went through two fun campaigns as a player before it was my turn to make a campaign of my own.

I never played *D&D* as a player ever again; I've only played as dungeon master since.

My first published game was *The Solo Dungeon*, in early 1978. It was a game book – a branching–story line game in which the player reads a paragraph, makes a decision, and then turns to a new paragraph pointed at by that decision to see what happened as a consequence and what new decision must now be made. It was one of the first such games published in the UK, and met with some success; sadly, it didn't meet with enough success to cover the heavy losses the publisher made on another game that led them to liquidation. I still have the unpublished second level of *The Solo Dungeon* sitting in my files, written in faded pencil.

The Solo Dungeon was different from its peers in two ways.

First, it had fragments of maps as some of its paragraphs so that the reader could stitch them together and build up a picture as they went along. Some of the map fragments were red herrings, to discourage people from taking sneak peeks at what might be awaiting them.

Second, the dungeon described by the text was narratively open ended. It was a place, rather than a story. Players didn't follow a single pathway, killing monsters that got in the way or that were in adjacent rooms: they could explore the dungeon at will. They had a freedom of movement that was not a feature of other game books at the time. I did make a mistake, in that I opened it up too much by (spoiler alert!) including a "Deck of Many Things". This was a pack of cards described in the *D&D* rule books, the use of which could introduce into the game world functionality over which I had no control and thus had no ability to cover in the paragraphs. One player contacted me and said his character had gone up six levels by drawing the right card from the Deck of Many Things, and he was a bit annoyed that he couldn't use any of the fancy spells that came with such advancement. This taught me a lesson about world design: each drop of reality that you allow to pass through the membrane that separates the imaginary from the real risks bursting it.

Roy Trubshaw never played *Dungeons & Dragons*. He did, however, play *ADVENT* (1976), one of the three games available on Essex University's DECsystem-10 (the other two being a *Star Trek* game and an empire-management game about being Hammurabi). The designation *ADVENT* came from what a maximum six-letter, capitals-only filename specification regime did to the name *Adventure*. Also known as *Colossal Cave Adventure*, *ADVENT* was text based with a command-line interface, as indeed operating systems had back then.

Roy later played *Zork* (1977) when a version temporarily became available on the university's mainframe. It had been translated into Fortran so as to run on DEC-10s and given the name *DUNGEN*. Because *DUNGEN* was manifestly better than *ADVENT*, Roy figured that in the future these games would all come to be called "dungeons". As things panned out, they were called "adventures" instead. The *D* in *MUD* stands for "dungeon" in this sense: Roy wanted to give people an idea of what *MUD* would be like before playing it and suggesting that it could be thought of as a multiplayer "dungeon" game would perhaps draw them in. I later tried calling MUDs MUAs, but the idea never took off. Whatever word players use to call something, that's what it's called. . . .

Roy was the first person at Essex University to finish *ADVENT*. He was also the first person there to finish *Zork*. This wasn't because he particularly enjoyed solving puzzles or playing games; it was because he sought better to understand how to build such pocket universes.

It was not, therefore, through simple spontaneity that Roy and I wrote *MUD*. A number of pieces had to be in place for it to happen. Because they were, though, it was inevitable that we would.

Roy's first attempt to create a world was only a brief prototype. In it, he allocated players what he called "genies", who were independent spirits under the player's control. These had some self-awareness and introduced themselves in terms of what they were genies of ("I am the genie of the watering can"). It was immediately clear to Roy that this didn't work as a conceit: the player felt too remote from the world if they interacted with it by telling a genie what to do and received first-person responses – "I see a chair" or "I open the door" or whatever.

For version 2 of the game, which Roy began work on immediately after testing the prototype, genies were gone. He kept the immediacy of the present tense, but described the world as is ("There is a chair here") and used second-person perspective to describe the player's actions ("You open the door"). Other players' actions were phrased using the third person ("Drahcir opens the door"). This put the player *in* the virtual world, rather than keeping them in the real world and interacting with it through a puppet.

Roy wanted a world that was separate from the real world, not part of it. He intended to flesh the world out enough to give players things to do. Goals and plans would emerge naturally from competitive or collaborative interactions between players, the world, and its contents. This is good enough for the real world, in which concepts such as experience points are not programmed in. Unfortunately, the computer on which *MUD* ran wasn't able to contain a world large enough or deep enough for such content to arise; it was like a stage with no show except what the audience put on itself.

I identified the design problem as being that there weren't enough ways for players to interact with one another, so there was little opportunity for drama. Drama, however, implied conflict, and Roy wasn't keen on that; he saw violence as one of the problems with the real world that he wanted to reject. He had deliberately not put combat into the game, and although some of us did add commands allowing players to one-shot certain nonplayer characters, we couldn't implement a full combat system. Incidentally, one creature I created in this period, the ox, still lives on decades later in *MUD2* with the vestiges of this functionality intact.

There were other things Roy did with *MUD* that I warned against, such as having a single key that was needed to enter a large area containing single-player, need-this-to-do-that puzzles. I'd played enough games that I could see what players would do: keep the key rather than return it for others to use after they'd explored the said area. Single-player puzzles weren't a great idea in the first place, come to that; Roy had added them to entertain the players, but he was conscious that it ran counter to the very multi-userness that was essential to the very concept of a fully fledged world.

These problems mounted. *MUD* had always been referred to as a game, and it never really occurred to us that, strictly speaking, it wasn't one. It became clear over the course of *MUD*'s first year, however, that we weren't going to be able to make the world rich enough that players would find things to do on their own: we were going to have to *give* them things to do. In other words, we would have to turn *MUD* into an actual game, in the sense of having its physics record and handle the players' scores. It would need game elements handled as "laws of nature" rather than as agreements between like-minded players as happens in real life.

The expression we used was that we'd have to "gamify" *MUD*. Somewhat confusingly for the modern reader, we used the term to mean turning *MUD* into a game, whereas today's usage means to add game elements *without* turning the target system into a game.

Following a long meeting about these problems, involving Roy, me, and two or three other hackers who later joined in, Roy made the decision to rewrite *MUD* as a full-on game.

Roy was not as experienced as me at game design, in that he had to work things out that to me were by now intuitive. We therefore did collaborate strongly on this, particularly with regard to the particular features the game would need. Surprisingly, this collaboration didn't extend to combat: while Roy was programming the communication system, he realized that he could just keep going and use the same principles for combat, so he did. Combat became a continuous turn-based but real-time exchange of blows between attacker and defender. It was only later that I was able to add the ability of players to act independently while this was going on, so they could strive to influence the outcome.

In real life, modulo certain religious beliefs, death is permanent. This was also to be the case in this third version of *MUD*, for two reasons. First, it was more realistic; indeed, we never even questioned the idea that player characters who were killed in combat would die. Second, if a player character was killed, the player could restart as a different character and play a different way, trying on a different identity.

Nevertheless, Roy did feel that it was perhaps a little unfair to consign player characters to oblivion for a single death; it might have arisen through accident or because the player didn't yet understand the game. He asked me what I thought about giving players a number of "lives". I believe the inspiration for this was pinball machines (of which most of us hackers were fans), where you began with a fixed number of balls (typically three or five) but could get extra balls through the course of play. The way Roy had implemented fighting, players exchanged blows with a random chance that they hit; when one did, then the suggestion was that either it would do no damage or it would knock a life off you.

I suggested that this solution was rather coarse and that we'd have better, more nuanced gameplay if we graduated the effects more. We could make each life be worth, say, 10 points and each blow do, say, 8–12 points; then there'd be some variation in how a fight could go, and players couldn't be sure how it would turn out; this would add excitement. It would also allow characters to recover points (which the original system didn't – if you lost a life, you never got it back). Linking fight outcomes to the experience point system we'd been mulling over meant that players would have a reason to stay, too, rather than simply running away as soon as combat began.

Giving players the opportunity to reboot their play as a new character if they were killed (that is, the second benefit we saw in permadeath) didn't really work initially. Players tended to play the game as themselves, rather than as imaginary selves, so when their character died, it made no difference to how they played when they came back. I realized that the cause of this was that they weren't role-playing. The problem wasn't necessarily that they hadn't encountered role-playing before, because it's not something that's hard to pick up – MUD practically shooed you in its direction; no, the issue was that players didn't believe they had *permission* to role-play. It was not part of the culture of the game, because it wasn't part of the culture of the real-life society in which they lived. They needed to be shown that MUD offered them a cultural shield, so that they could pretend to be someone else without fear of mockery.

Because I had a background in role-playing, I concocted a scheme to introduce the idea.

When I took over code ownership of MUD, Roy hadn't yet implemented gender. He had very little time left to work on MUD but a great deal he needed to implement before passing control to me; he didn't see gender as important, so he left that for me to do as an exercise, to help me learn my way around his code. He had to implement at least one gender (because the English language required it) and went with male; this was because he'd written all the documentation referring to the user as female, so having male characters balanced this. Besides, the demographics of computer science departments being what they were, almost all the players were in practice male anyway, so he'd get less grief this way.

When I took over the code, I created a debug character to use: Polly. The name was chosen ostensibly because it's archetypical for parrots, but in actuality because it's a female name. This meant that when I added to MUD the option for characters to be female, Polly was naturally going to be female. I could then play Polly as a cheerful, feisty young woman who was helpful but didn't suffer fools gladly. The other players knew I was me; they also knew I was Polly; they knew how I played as Polly was not how I played as me; they knew that my playing as not-me was permissible; they realized that their playing as not-them was also permissible; they played as not-them.

Thenceforth, people could and almost always did role-play in MUD. This freed them up to explore different facets of themselves, as intended.

Roy didn't put much content at all in this MUD version 3 (that is, MUD1). He put in just enough to test that the language he had designed for specifying the world, MUDDL, could indeed be used to specify a world. He didn't have the time to invest much effort in building the said world, though. That fell entirely to me.

I could have chosen any setting that I wanted for the game. There were no precedents, and there was no competition: people were going to play MUD for its gameplay however I dressed it up, so I had a free choice. I considered several possibilities – *Three Musketeers*-era France, the world of Scheherazade, escaping from a prisoner of war camp, the Camelot of Arthurian legend – but I settled on what today would be called high fantasy. The world Roy had designed for version 2 had had elements of this, but it was whimsical – more *Alice in Wonderland* (1865) or *The Lion, the Witch and the Wardrobe* (1950) than *The Lord of the Rings*. I liked the idea of starting out whimsically, but I wanted the game to become tauter as players advanced. High fantasy gave me that.

I didn't think of it as any kind of fantasy, though: to me, it was folklore (in particular, English folklore). Fantasy *was* a term in use back then, but not one I'd come across much – I'd encountered sword and sorcery as a genre name far more often. Folklore was something different, though: it was understood by people almost at an intuitive level, but not in its details. It was therefore familiar in the abstract but unfamiliar in the specific; it allowed for the introduction of a sense of disquiet, so the player knew what *might* be, but not what *was*. It let me mirror the resonance and dissonance that players would feel with respect to their character, that in some sense it *was* them but in others it *wasn't*, and that their aim was to harmonize the two. I may have been only 20 at this point, but I did know what I wanted the game to say and how I could say it.

That my interpretation of English folklore would today be classified as high fantasy is perhaps no coincidence. The absolutely archetypical example of high fantasy is J. R. R. Tolkien's work *The Lord of the Rings*. Tolkien drew on his extensive knowledge and understanding of English folklore to create the foundations of his world, Middle-earth. My own understanding came from the books of Enid Blyton and the Rupert Bear annuals I would receive as a present each Christmas as a child; it would never be as deep as Tolkien's, obviously, but the truths I discerned were the same.

Tolkien spent April 1917 to October 1918 recuperating from trench fever in East Yorkshire, where he was assigned to spend his days staring out over the Holderness cliffs at the sea, looking for signs of invasion. Half a century later, I would spend many hours looking out from my bedroom window over those same cliffs at that same sea, having those same thoughts about building my own world just over the horizon of what we think of as the real.

English folklore allowed me to do something else with *MUD* that I perhaps couldn't have done with some of the other genres I considered. Because it wasn't nailed down to a particular time, it meant I could use time as a metaphor for danger. Players could in theory wander anywhere they wanted to in the game, so I needed a way of warning those with little experience that they might be about to go somewhere they could come to wish they hadn't. By associating time with danger, I could do that. The game started in an area reminiscent of the 1930s, which I inherited from Roy: a gravedigger's cottage. Further afield, I put an inn from the late Victorian era, a tin mine from perhaps the 1700s, a 1500s galleon at sea, a 1200s oriental temple, and (the most dangerous place in the land) a ring of stones dating from prehistory. I never told players that I was using this history-as-danger metaphor, but they did seem to sense it and its success greatly exceeded my expectations.

There were symbolic reasons for wanting to use this particular metaphor, too. These took me awhile to understand, because although I knew I did *want* this metaphor, I couldn't really articulate *why* except by implementing it. Eventually – perhaps two or three years after implementing the concept – I concluded that the reason was to do with remoteness from the present. The older something is, the more primitive it is, and the closer to independence it is. By gradually stripping away the physical and societal protections of modern life, the chains that hold a player in place are also shed, one by one, until eventually the player is free. Because the past equated to danger, and danger equated to advancement, the past equated to advancement; more to the point, advancement equated to the past.

In short, I chose the fictional genre for *MUD* because of the symbolism it afforded me, and I designed the world in service of that symbolism. However, I also designed it in service to gameplay, because the whole point of gamifying *MUD* was to encourage people to play it as a game.

Roy and I had discussed how players might advance in this game. As players played, they would grow in their experience of the game; we needed their characters to reflect that growth in order to show players that we recognized and so validated it. The most obvious way was to award characters points that tracked the growth of their players. Roy proposed this idea and was quite amused when I told him that this was how *D&D* did it with its experience points system.

By the time it came to implementing the concept, I had to do it all myself. I included something else I had come across in *D&D*: levels. Levels added extra oomph to experience points, because they provided clear goals. A certain number of experience points would get a character to the next level, which provided the player with an achievable intermediate target. With no levels, the distance from zero points to the maximum could have looked daunting, but with levels, it was broken down into manageable chunks. It also allowed step-change rewards such as spell acquisition and stat changes to be associated with going up a level, so boosting the sense of achievement associated with leveling up.

I knew that this would work because I'd seen it do so in *D&D*; *D&D* itself derived the concept of levels (and in a less refined form, experience points) from its war-games heritage.

Levels weren't the only way I could have done it, of course. I could, for example, simply have stuck with experience points. If I'd awarded a new spell at 10,000 experience points, say, then people would have treated round numbers of experience points (rather than levels) as attainable targets. It would have meant that stat increases could have been spread out more (strength is some base value plus your current experience point total divided by a constant), which would in turn have smoothed the gameplay out more. Additionally, I could have implemented an ability system, allowing players to cash in experience points for gains in functionality of particular importance to them as individuals, instead of a one-size-fits-all.

I could have separated abilities from experience by introducing a task system so that if you wanted to cast the summon spell, then you'd have to have read that one really-hard-to-reach book that taught you it. I could have based it on gear, as modern MMOs do in their elder game period (not ideally, because it conflates who you are with what you possess).

I could have completely ignored experience points and introduced a skill system. Skill systems were a recent innovation in tabletop role-playing games, most notably employed by *Traveler* (1977) and *RuneQuest* (1978); the jury was still out as to whether the full range of players would like them or not, though, and I didn't want to risk that they might flop. I knew experience points plus levels would do the business and were both simple enough for new players to understand and graduated enough for longer-term players to appreciate; that's therefore what I went with for *MUD*. We didn't have the time available for play-testing to do much else anyway.

The same sort of design ideals were applied everywhere else in the game. The geography, the mobiles, the way magic worked, the (deliberate lack of an) economy – everything was constructed to be in tune, so it was all saying the same thing to the player: this is a self-contained reality which is, and for a long time will continue to be, fun.

So concludes this summary of the origins of *MUD* mythologized in terms of the design that went into its creation. The history of making imaginary worlds; the crisis of not being able to deliver what was hoped for; the rewrite that turned things around; the design metaphors employed; the mechanics, either created originally or consciously copied from other games; the consistency of the design with the designers' shared vision: so it is that virtual worlds began.

To the best of my recollection, all this is correct.

It's historically correct, in terms of its description of the events that happened and the order in which they happened. It's causally correct, in that each event described led to what is claimed to be a consequence.

It doesn't describe *MUD*'s origins at all.

As Art

The 2017 UK City of Culture was Kingston upon Hull.

The main point of the City of Culture award is to give a city that's completely lacking in culture a taste of what it's missing. I remember listening to a radio program at the end of the year in which people from Hull were asked whether they thought its being UK City of Culture had made a difference. The consensus was that it was fun while it lasted, but no, it hadn't. Hull was the end of the line. There was nothing beyond it.

Those people (such as me) who grew up some distance "beyond" Hull didn't see it like that at all. From the perspective of a small seaside town an hour's bus ride away, Hull wasn't the end of the line; it was the beginning. We were provincial, but Hull was the glamorous metropolis.

Hull was actually no such thing. It was the second-most bombed city in Britain in World War II (after London), and its center had been speedily rebuilt in unsympathetic, brutalist concrete. It was as dead end as its residents thought it was and was itself provincial when looked at from the perspective of Leeds or even York, which in turn were provincial when viewed from London.

It used to be that my hometown was the largest in the country not to have a class-A road running to it. With a population of around 8,000, it was twice as big as the next town bearing this distinction. That's since changed, with the redesignation of a B road; the road itself hasn't changed, however; only the road signs have, to reflect its new name. There's little point upgrading them for a place no one goes to, that they only come from.

For me, then, as a child growing up, there was nothing to the east but sea and nothing to the west but a city that was ranked number 1 in the country in a 2003 survey to find "Britain's crappiest town".

Basically, then, I come from nowhere.

My father was a gas fitter. His job was installing domestic gas appliances in people's homes. My mother was a school meals cook. Her job was producing enough food to satisfy several hundred children every day. It was unusual for married women to be employed in those days, but not in my hometown. Most had a job, because otherwise the family wouldn't be able to get by.

We were poor, but we didn't really know we were because everyone was. I had a very happy childhood.

As I grew older, though, I began to appreciate that something wasn't right. I'd see people on TV being lauded for having talents that were exceeded by those of my friends at my school. I saw respect being given to individuals not for who they were, but for whose children they were. I saw a world of luxury being presented as the norm and realized that it actually *was* the norm: most other people really did live like that. Conversely, I looked around my council estate and saw nothing like it reflected on TV. It seemed that in other parts of the country, girls didn't go around in thick tights as outerwear because their one skirt was in the wash: they had more than one skirt. Teenagers wore jeans without patches on the knees. Their houses had telephones.

They didn't speak with my accent, either.

I came to the conclusion that the world wasn't fair.

I also concluded that, given my station in life, I was unlikely to be able to change this state of affairs either for people in general or for me in particular.

My father was a gamer. He encouraged my brother and me to play games, too. Every weekend, we'd play several board games or card games together. He never said no to us when we asked, and we asked a lot. After every game of *Monopoly* (1935) that we finished, he recorded the winner on the back of a £500 note. When those ran out, he moved to the £100 notes. When those ran out, he started again on the £500s, writing the new results beneath the old ones. We played *Risk* (1957) 96 times in total, of which I won on only one occasion – the 96th. We had dozens of board games in the end, mainly manufactured by Waddington's. My dad would go to Hull especially to get them. We always had a new one to look forward to on November 5, in lieu of fireworks (which were more expensive and didn't last as long) and at Christmas.

My mother was a storyteller. She made up stories herself just to tell me and my brother, and she'd adapt them in the telling depending on our reactions. Her stories were therefore always perfect, because they were individualized for us in the moment. She set her stories in a magical world that overlaid the real world. There were places where our world and the world of pixies were close, where we could see these little figures going about their business. She wove in elements of the stories she'd heard herself as a child – not in terms of their narratives, but in their allusions to Fairyland.

We may have lived in a world of deprivation, but we *lived* in our imaginations.

Today, around half of UK teenagers go to university. In 1978, it was around one in seven. Then, as now, people from a poor, working-class background were the least likely to find themselves the beneficiaries of a higher education.

I was smart, though – *very* smart. I managed to pass my exams through flair alone and won a place at Essex University to study mathematics. I switched at the end of the first year to computer science; of the 300 students taking maths, two got higher marks than me, but none were close in computing.

I was expecting the other students to be supersmart too, but they were no different to the kids I knew from home; indeed, most of them would have been merely average in comparison. The difference was that they had had opportunities that my regular school friends hadn't.

The exceptions were the other people taking computer science. Some of those were also very smart and had backgrounds similar to mine. Britain, it transpired, anticipated a future need for software engineers, and because few middle-class children were prepared to sully their hands with the subject, it was possible for working-class kids to get to places on computer science degrees. Along with a handful of middle-class students who loved computing enough to take it in defiance of their parents' wishes, we formed a merry band who took to computers for the sheer, unadulterated freedom they offered.

Freedom was indeed *exactly* what some of us wanted.

We'd started our lives situated by accidents of birth. We'd been defined by others, not by ourselves. We were in a world of injustice and unfairness over which we had no influence, nor any prospect of influence. Other students looked down on us. We, however, shared visions of the future that we had brought with us from our preuniversity world; we were excited and overjoyed that others shared those visions.

For some few of us, those visions were specific, powerful, and very compelling.

We couldn't change the world, but we didn't care. We could make our *own* worlds that were better.

This is what Roy and I were doing with *MUD*. The "real" world needed some competition, and that's what it was going to get.

In the past, the poor and downtrodden put their faith in imagined heavens – afterlives that were promised them, that they believed in because they needed to know that there must be *something* better. We, however, could offer a new world in the here and now. Reality stank. We were angry, and we were going to make a new reality that freed us from reality's limitations, shackles, and constraints. We could be who we *were*, not who others wanted us to be.

This is why Roy was looking for alternatives to inter-process communication calls. It wasn't out of mere curiosity – he had a reason to wish access to them: he wanted to make a better world, literally. He didn't want to make the real world better: he wanted to make a world that was better than the real world. When he found that he could write to the high segment, it was a metaphor for all that he hoped to achieve: change that which people thought to be unchangeable. This is why he planned to make a world that was separate from the real world, not part of it. It wasn't an idea that came out of nowhere: it had purpose.

He made his world with lifelike physics so that people would understand how it worked. He was hoping that it would be a living world that changed and evolved as people played, but his dreams exceeded what the DECsystem-10 could handle. He couldn't make a world either big enough or deep enough for this purpose. He knew he'd have to rewrite it, but what caused him to rewrite it as a game is because life is a game. Unlike life, however, this would be a game that any and all could win.

We encouraged other people to write their own MUDs not because we particularly believed in free software (although we did); rather, it was because this followed our agenda of giving people alternatives to reality. The more virtual worlds there were, the more people could play them. The more people could play them, the freer people as a whole could be. They could become, then be, themselves.

I put the concept of virtual worlds into the public domain because I didn't want anyone owning it, including me. If I'd died or gone bankrupt and someone had acquired the rights to the game, they could have used it as the basis of a patent. That would have led to the exact opposite situation to the one that Roy and I wanted.

I'd made many self-contained worlds when I was young. There were at least three other long-term projects that I and my brother engaged in before I created Dr Toddystone. Unlike my brother, I'd also made board games – indeed, I still make board games every once in a while. When you make a game, you learn what it is you want to say and how to say it. Its mechanics are your language; its gameplay, your message.

We had access to a computer in my school, over a 110 baud modem. This may seem odd, given what I've just said about how remote the place was, but perversely, this remoteness worked to its advantage. British Petroleum had a chemical works nearby that disgorged clouds of who-knows-what in our direction, and the company made school access to its mainframe available as a public-relations exercise (which worked; they did come across as decent people). I used the computer, found programming an easy concept to grasp, and wrote games for it for fun. When I worked on *MUD*, I'd written more computer games than I had played. Nevertheless, of all the possibilities computers offered, I knew that ultimately I wanted to use one to implement a world – and it was dawning on me why, too.

I'd seen *ADVENT* before I came to Essex, in the form of a transcript published in *Bellicus*, a postal games magazine to which I subscribed. The interface was like that of a BASIC program I'd written called *Talker*, which carried on a conversation with the user. I'd written *Talker* to see if I could create plausible nonplayer characters; I could, but it soon ran out of things to say. I later did a PhD in artificial intelligence for exactly the same reason.

I came to Essex University hoping to use a computer to write a world and was filled with glee when I joined the Computer Society and found that Roy had embarked on this very quest just a few days earlier.

When it fell to me to become primary author of *MUD*, I had to decide what setting to use. In my teens, I and two of my gamer friends from school had made a board game – *Wizards & Heroes*, it was called, and it was based on an idea described in the magazine *Games and Puzzles* (1972–1981, 1994–1996) to which my father subscribed. I'd taken it through several iterations and explored some of the milieux known to me at the time. I was aware from that what English folklore would let me do. It wasn't just a setting nor even just a world that touched ours in ways both known and unknown: it had rules and mechanics. When certain things happened, other things also had to happen; the reader merely had a say in *how* they happened.

Folklore – high fantasy – adapted itself to conform to the reader, to which the reader could then respond; this took both the story and the reader in exactly the direction they both wanted to go. The same could be said of any oral tradition, of course, but this one I'd actually experienced (via my mother). Furthermore, hours of staring out at the sea, spinning tales for myself, had equipped me not only with the tools to construct stories but with an understanding of what I wanted to construct with them. I too wished to make a world that was better than the one into which I was born.

I went with levels in my design for *MUD1* because of the British class system.

In Britain, many things affect your ability to progress in society. Gender, skin color, age, sexuality, disability level – all are factors. They mainly have their roots in biology, although in the case of disability, physics too can play a part (you can be in a wheelchair through illness or accident). It can also be reasonably argued that some, such as gender, are to various degrees social constructs, albeit with a genetic basis.

Class is entirely a social construct.

Class is pervasive and dreadful – absolutely dreadful. Anyone brought up in the UK knows within moments of observing or hearing you what class you are. It's something you're pretty well locked into at birth, and social mobility is therefore very difficult to achieve. Even today, I may well be a learned professor, but as soon as I talk to people outside academia I may as well be a peasant.

Roy and I were not *at all* happy with this state of affairs. It made us seethe. So it was that when I was deciding how to have *MUD* recognize the advancement of the player, I was specifically aiming to use the opportunity to tear into the class system, exposing and correcting its flaws.

This is why I chose levels. Levels were like classes in the British class system. I had a limited number of them – a dozen or so – and I gave them all names (and thus a personality). If you saw that someone was a sorcerer or a heroine, you knew immediately what their social standing was. The critical difference was that you could *rise* through the levels if you had sufficient ability and strength of character – which everybody *did* have, if only they could see it. *MUD* helped them to see it. Outside *MUD*, you were whoever others decreed you were; inside *MUD*, the mechanics were geared so that you could be whoever *you* decreed you were. All you had to do was to realize that.

This was a political statement. That made it an artistic statement. *MUD* was Roy's and my response to the prevailing social order.

This use of the game to make political and artistic statements was extensive. For example, *MUD* was constrained to be textual in nature, therefore was beholden to the English language. The English language necessitates gendered pronouns. Roy and I were resolutely against gender as a concept: people were people, and that was that. Gender shouldn't matter. If we could have written *MUD* without gender, we would have. Roy tried removing it in the rewrite for version 3, but the text always read too stiltedly artificial. When I created Polly, yes, I was showing players how to role-play – but I was also making it explicit that gender wasn't a thing. I initialized new characters differently based on their sex (+10 strength for male, +5 dexterity and stamina for female) precisely so that these differences would be erased as the characters went up levels and the values hit the cap of 100 (around level 5 or 6). I was saying through this that how you were born was one thing, but what you became wasn't dependent on that. I added easy ways for characters to change gender, through spells and magical artifacts, and inserted a couple of gender-specific puzzles that gave players gameplay reasons for wanting to do so. Many is the occasion that a player forgot what gender their character currently was and had to check their profile to find out.

So concludes this summary of the origins of *MUD* mythologized in terms of the art that went into its creation. The disenchantment with reality, the desire to improve on it, the yearning for freedom, the actualization of identity, the critique of 1970s Britain: so it is that virtual worlds began.

To the best of my recollection, all this is correct.

It's historically correct, in terms of its description of the events that happened and the order in which they happened. It's causally correct, in that each event described led to what is claimed to be a consequence.

It doesn't describe *MUD*'s origins at all.

Interpretation

Stories change in the retelling. People take from them what they want or need and propagate them emphasizing what they feel is important. Games, as with oral stories, change in the playing, so that stories can be changed not only in the retelling but in the telling itself.

As craft, as design, as art: I've used all three of these origin stories for *MUD* and continue to do so as appropriate. All of them capture the essence of the game's creation, doing so in ways meaningful to different audiences.

Roy and I didn't discuss any of this much; we didn't have the philosophical education to articulate it anyway. We understood it implicitly, not explicitly. The longest discussion we ever had on the topic of what *MUD* should be concerned the transformation from *MUD* version 2 to version 3; this was several hours long and ultimately involved two or three other members of the Computer Society, too. Everything else was in snatches no more than five or ten minutes long at most. I might ask Roy why he was doing something a particular way, but I never asked why he was doing it in the first place – I never needed to, because in my view it was always the right thing to be aiming to do anyway. We simply *knew* what we wanted, and there was little point in talking about it, as we also knew we both wanted the same thing. We had the same motives; we were both capable: we just did it.

Essex University wasn't my first choice. If it had been explained to me how examination scripts were marked, I wouldn't have passed on flair alone and would have wound up at Exeter or conceivably Cambridge.

What if Roy and I hadn't met?

Roy would have written the prototype and gone on to do version 2. When it came to version 3, however, he'd have floundered. He didn't have the game design background, and he didn't have the time to finish it. *MUD* would have been an historical curiosity that would have been revealed years later as being "the first" virtual world, but its impact would have been zero on today's MMORPGs. It would have been a precursor, but not a progenitor.

I would have written a virtual world if I'd had access to a mainframe, but I wouldn't have been able to start until I'd acquired the necessary programming expertise. I'd probably have wanted to rewrite it after a year too, and would have also found myself pressed for time. I would, however, have been able to finish it, assuming I stayed on to do a PhD, but by then one of the other early worlds – *Sceptre of Goth*, most likely – would have been the breakthrough product. I wouldn't have cared about this, because I wouldn't have been doing it to be "first" (as it was, Roy and I didn't know that there weren't already dozens of games like *MUD* out there already when we started). Nevertheless, I wouldn't have been the person writing this essay if I hadn't gone to Essex University and met Roy Trubshaw.

It was a case of right place, right time, then.

Roy remains somewhat bemused by the success of *MUD*. He had dreams when he started but hadn't anticipated that they'd actually begin to come true. I myself am more frustrated: I know what we were trying to achieve, but as more people wrote virtual worlds based on *MUD* (or, more likely, its descendants), its message was denuded. Few designers today have the freedom to speak to their players through their designs even if they want to, and this is a terrible shame.

MUD was the *product* of craft, design, and art, but it *wasn't* any of them. It was an ideal. This gives me hope: the worlds have changed, but the ideal remains as strong as it ever was. We were always going to get virtual worlds, because the ideal was always going to emerge, and it will continue to reemerge until it is met. Humanity is only at the start – possibly a false one – of a long, long journey. When it arrives there, though, what wonders will await us!

If you want the most accurate mythologization of *MUD*'s origins, then, I am happy to express it in one, simple word.

That word is *luck*.

3

ROCKALL

A Liminal, Transauthorial World Founded on the Atlantis Myth

Mark Sebanc

In a remarkable passage, strikingly paradoxical, C. J. Jung avers that "in general, it is the non-psychological novel that offers the richest opportunities for psychological elucidation". He explains that it is precisely by avoiding a prejudiced narrative that views the world through a psychological lens that the door is opened to analysis and interpretation. He goes on to discuss H. Rider Haggard, the romantic storyteller of the late Victorian and Edwardian period, as an exemplary exponent of such fiction, which he calls visionary, praising the insights to be gained from an exciting tale like *She: A History of Adventure* (1886) or *Ayesha: The Return of She* (1905), inasmuch as it "is constructed against a background of unspoken psychological assumptions, and the more unconscious the author is of them, the more this background reveals itself in unalloyed purity to the discerning eye".[1] One is reminded here of a lapidary line from Ovid's *Ars Amatoria* (2 AD), "*Si latet, ars prodest*", which is to say that art is most effective when it is latent or hidden.[2]

Such illusive latency marks the deceptively simple narrative lineaments of Bill Sarjeant's imaginary continent of Rockall, but not his richly articulated world-building, patently ambitious and comprehensive in its amplitude. The world of Rockall is indeed an entirely unique accomplishment, one that befits the exceptional gifts of its creator, who demonstrated an uncommon ability to straddle the two cultures famously adumbrated by C. P. Snow.

As well as being the author of a 12-novel cycle centered on Rockall and titled *The Perilous Quest for Lyonesse*, the late Professor William Antony Swithin (Bill) Sarjeant was a palynologist, paleontologist, ichnologist, historian of geology, field naturalist, archivist, bibliophile, local historian, folk singer, musicologist, and Sherlockian scholar – the very paragon of an astonishingly polymathic versatility, a consummate example, in the apothegmatic words of Jacob Bronowski, of the deeper, more comprehensive epistemological truth that, "Man is unique not because he does science, and he is unique not because he does art, but because science and art equally are expressions of his marvelous plasticity of mind".[3] Not only that, but Sarjeant was also the scion of an older world, now removed from us by a profound gulf not so much of time as of metaphysical temper and outlook.

The first four novels in the Rockall series, now out of print, were published in the 1990s by HarperCollins UK, while six remain in manuscript. The 11th novel is partially written, and the 12th exists only in the form of preliminary notes. This is how Sarjeant describes the creative origins of his alternative world of Rockall, an imaginary island continent situated northwest of the British Isles in the North Atlantic and named eponymously after a tiny islet only 20 meters in size situated on an oceanic plateau:

> When I was a child, Rockall was not claimed by any nation, nor could I dis-
> cover anything about it. This lack of information fired my youthful imagi-
> nation, so that soon I had worked out the geography of Rockall, its animal
> and plant life, and even its history and present-day politics; I had decided on
> its sports and its heraldry, and I made quite detailed maps of my imaginary
> island. After neglecting my island for more than 25 years, I returned to it in
> my 40s and made large scale, detailed maps of its physical features, geology,
> botany and ethnology, its present geography and even its political constitu-
> encies. . . . Eventually, upon urging from my wife, I began actually to write
> my long-planned novels.[4]

Sarjeant was a man of brilliantly multifarious parts, a Renaissance man of manifest genius. In 1992, for example, on the occasion of the centenary of Tolkien's birth, he delivered a paper at Oxford on the geology of Middle-earth.[5] In another paper, "The Shire: Its Bounds, Food and Farming", published just a year before his death, in his typically painstaking, comprehensive fashion, Sarjeant delved into the socio-economic structure of Tolkien's hobbit homeland.[6] Even back in the 1990s, when the books in the series were first launched under less than ideal circumstances of editorial input and correction, there was a sense that he had achieved something that bore comparison to Tolkien in its scope and range. For instance, in tribute to Sarjeant, there are geophysical features of the suboceanic Rockall Plateau that have been named after locations in his novels (e.g., Lyonesse, Owlsgard, Sandastre), as though his Rockall, which deliberately draws on the Atlantis myths, had merely sunk beneath the waves. Further to the southwest, in close proximity to these place names derived from Sarjeant, you can find similar undersea features named after locations from *The Lord of the Rings* (1954–1955): Edoras Bank, Gondor Seamount, Gandalf's Spur.

Apart from the prologue, the 12-novel series is set entirely at a time that is coextensive with our own Middle Ages and at more or less the same technological level, even though, in Sarjeant's broader conception, Rockall is a world that has a history roughly concurrent with our own, extending even to modern times.

This focal aspect of Sarjeant's world-building demonstrates the enduring allure of the Middle Ages as a cynosure of nostalgic yearning, a predilection with strong undercurrents that extends back to the Romantic period, most notably with Sir Walter Scott.[7] The first quartet of novels in the series consists of the following titles: *Princes of Sandastre, The Lords of the Stoney Mountains, The Winds of the Wastelands,* and *The Nine Gods of Safaddné.*

At the outset, HarperCollins UK had exceedingly high hopes for the success of this ambitious project, but the series did not catch on, not least because of some of its deficiencies of narrative structure and certain other blemishes in terms of literary workmanship, but for all that these are overshadowed by the sheer expansive brilliance of the world-building. In many ways, one could say of Sarjeant's work what Henry James famously said of Tolstoy's *War and Peace* (1869), that it was a "loose baggy monster", impressively large and imposing, but disfigured by what Samuel Johnson might have called anfractuosities of style and pacing. For example, there is a frequent recurrence of rhetorical questions on the part of the first-person narrator that becomes somewhat cloying as well as a tendency to indulge in long information dumps that act to impede the flow of the story. Hence, in the original version, the first novel in the cycle is tediously slow in unfolding. As prodigiously gifted as he was and as brilliant an academic as he was, Sarjeant was still in a phase of apprenticeship, still on a learning curve in terms of the novelist's craft. In any case, as a result, the series foundered and was abandoned in its earlier stages, an outcome hastened by Sarjeant's untimely death from liver cancer on July 8, 2002.

After Sarjeant's passing, all further progress on the project was effectively and seemingly permanently forestalled. As a novelist and writer, I myself had corresponded with Sarjeant after having serendipitously bought a copy of *Princes of Sandastre* (1990) not long after its publication. This led me to his series, and soon I came to have a vivid sense of the virtuosity and magnitude of his achievement. In our exchange of communications, we had also expressed a mutual admiration for one another's work. From our long-distance relationship (we never met each other in person), I knew as well that there were novels in the Rockall series unpublished that he had left in the manuscript. In the years following his untimely death, I had always harbored the feeling in the back of my mind that it would be a tragedy if Bill's splendid body of literary work, with its altogether unique world-building, were to die as a stillbirth, which is why I lobbied vigorously for its resurrection and why his estate accorded me the honor and privilege of editing and rewriting the original text.

In the foreword to the original edition of *Princes of Sandastre*, Sarjeant sets the *mise-en-scène* for the series, laying out the governing conceit of his alternative continent of Rockall. He imagines it as half as big as Australia, a real present-day island nation in our actual world, but one that is fiercely isolationist and off the beaten track, agrarian and anachronistically out of step with consumerist modernity, a place of "less noise and more green" to use the words of Tolkien. At the same time, for all its bucolically utopian complexion, it is a place that is not exempt from the vicissitudes of the human condition.

In this foreword, Sarjeant describes the Republic of Rockall as "one of the wealthiest countries on earth" and explains that it "remains remarkably little known. Its unique flora and fauna arouse profound interest among naturalists and its rocks condition the thinking of geologists about the structure of the whole North Atlantic basin; yet few naturalists or geologists have been fortunate enough to visit this sea-girt realm". Sarjeant continues,

> Rockall is in many ways an unusual country. Its eight-house parliament is a model for study by political scientists, yet the operations of that parliament are little understood in other democracies and nowhere emulated. It continues to rely upon animal power and steam haulage for road and rail transportation and employs battery-powered helicopters for emergency services and for recreation. Petroleum is used only to power long-distance aeroplanes. . . .
>
> Of all European countries, Rockall has the fewest roads, the most green countryside, the most benign and unspoiled shores, the least trodden and most challenging mountains; yet of all countries, it welcomes tourists from abroad least. . . .
>
> Geographically, Rockall is the farthest-flung of European countries, isolated by the turbulent Atlantic from the expansionist ambitions of kings and the greedy philosophies of clerics and republics. Even during the present century [that is, the 20th century], Rockall has remained a country apart. The First World War certainly produced serious upheavals in the nascent republic, yet outside involvements were largely avoided; and whilst, in the Second World War, Rockall did play a major role in the struggle against the fascist powers, afterwards it withdrew again within its own bounds.[8]

It is all too evident that, in a world rendered increasingly small by the advent of GPS and the satellite imaging of every nook and cranny of the earth, such a proposition beggars credibility. In the new rendition of the series, now forthcoming from the English publisher, Gollancz, in keeping with my commission from the Sarjeant Estate to revise the novels, my first order of business, given the manifest implausibility of conceiving of Rockall as a real, but undiscovered, nation in our world, was to provide a completely new framing idea or device for the project. To this end, I have created a new and original 7,000-word prologue titled "The Portal", which acts now as an introduction to the whole series. Essentially a short story and set in the modern day, it postulates the reality of a kind of wormhole in the North Atlantic that has opened and closed over the ages, providing desultory entry into Rockall, which is now imagined as an alternative version of a portion of our world that exists in another dimension, even while it retains certain spatial coordinates coextensive with our own. In this prologue, I have employed the classic narrative stratagem of the "recovered manuscript" as the basis for the long sequence of books that follow, all of them set in a period that coincides temporally with our own 15th century.

Beyond this new introductory frame, the novels will have been extensively rewritten and overhauled in terms of style, pacing, and description, with new and original scenes being grafted onto the original narrative. Because they are incomplete or fragmentary as they now stand, the last two novels in the sequence will likely bear the more definitive stamp of my own workmanship. At this time, Gollancz has contracted to publish the initial quartet of titles in the series, beginning with the first and second novels (*Princes of Sandastre* and *The Lords of the Stoney Mountains*).

Consisting of a number of different nations and peoples, Rockall also has its own rather distinctive flora and fauna, many of these suggestive of our own earth's prehistory. As is revealed in *Princes of Sandastre* by way of backstory, Rockall is the remnant northern portion of a larger continent, once under the sway of an oppressive, totalitarian people whose hegemony ended when they were overwhelmed in a cataclysmic natural event. As mentioned earlier, Sarjeant himself construes this continent as Atlantis.

On his original, now-defunct website, Sarjeant speaks of Rockall as a "land wreathed in legend; a land of weird beasts and wondrous happenings, of great beauties and terrible dangers". Apart from a number of offshore islands, its main landmass, he explains, is "shaped roughly like a broad-waisted hourglass. It comprises four major regions: the Northern Mountains, the Eastern Mountains, the Central Lowlands and the Southern Mountains".

Sarjeant goes on, moreover, to describe Rockall's flora and fauna:

> There are coniferous forests enough in the Old and New Worlds, but the forests of northwestern Rockall are quite different. The bizarre wind-forests of northern Reschora and Kelcestre are without parallel. As for the mighty peveneks of Sandastre, their like is to be found only among the giant redwoods of California.
>
> The forests of the lower northern hills and of central and southern Rockall are deciduous, like those of Europe. However, they, too, exhibit many differences. Not all are obvious, but any visitor would be surprised by the scaly-trunked skarens with their pale leaves, the russet-red trunks of the toronots of the West Marches, and the saffron-flowered ebelmeks of Sandastre.
>
> The flora of the Great Marshes at the Aramassa's mouth is wholly unique from the misshapen catumat trees, through the tallavarry reeds (for so long important in Rockall's economy), down to the smallest marsh plants. Even the plants of the smaller, inland marshes and peat mosses show strong differences from those elsewhere.

Though Rockall is at the heart of an ocean, not all of it is humid. It has a desert, albeit small in extent, and there are other regions whose aridity results from situation and rock type. Each of these has plants unique to it, which are often of high commercial value. Rockall does have green grasslands: for example, the Green River of Herador has shores as green as any in England. However, nowhere else are there grasslands yellow at all seasons, like those of Montariot; nowhere else are there red grasslands, like those of the Serren Lowlands; nowhere else is there anything to match the grey-green soudredge (soderag) moors of Vragansarat.

With so different a flora, it is not surprising to find a fauna just as remarkable. While amphibians and reptiles of Rockall show, in general, strong relationships with those elsewhere, there are also notable differences. The chelonians – members of the turtle family – may attain exceptional size, like the glagrangs of the Aramassa river system. The Great Marshes have many unusual reptiles, including crocodiles of the archaic type and snakes with unusual abilities. In the arid Mentone Hills, lizards grow to greater size than their relatives in Europe. Fiery-skinned salamanders and gliding frogs are among many other Rockalese specialties.

Some of the birds have much in common with those in Europe and North America. The taron of the northern shores is much like the gannet; the gherek of the Northern Mountains differs only in colour from large falcons; and the rewlen of central Rockall is much like a raven.

However, the plumage of Rockall's small birds is more often green than brown and, in most other groups, the Rockalese species are unique, even if their behaviour is not. An especially striking difference is that Rockall boasts no owls; instead, their role is taken up by night-flying falcons.

It is in the mammals that the greatest differences are found. Of course, there are creatures equivalent to the mammals of the rest of the world: the bavalins of southern Rockall and kalvaks of central Rockall are much like rhinoceroses; the galikhu like a water-hog, the aruchin much like a goat and the danatel like an antelope the size of a jackrabbit. Such carnivores as the thassak of southern Rockall and the branath of the north are comparable to lions and tigers, while amerals are much like lesser predators such as ermines or minks. However, in other cases, the differences are profound. To find parallels to such creatures as the selth or the scaunt of central Rockall or the tasdavari, xalenth and udru of the Northern Mountains, one must look far back in geological time.

The most remarkable feature is the capability of a number of Rock-alese mammals to form telepathic links with each other and also, to a variable extent according to their intelligence, with humans. A whole group of horned antelope-like creatures have this. It is weakest, perhaps, in the hasedu, an animal that, because it yields milk and because of its strength in hauling, serves the purpose in Rockall that cattle serve elsewhere. The animals used for riding all have stronger telepathic powers: they include the sevdru of southern Rockall, the rafenu of the central forests and the sturdy veledu and unicorn-like xalihu of the Northern Mountains. The larger and much rarer remora (dakhramar) is possessed of the greatest telepathic powers, but it has not formed any regular relationship with mankind.

Comparably strong telepathic powers are exhibited voluntarily by the vasian of the forests of southern Rockall, an arboreal creature much like the tarsier of Indonesia and the Philippines. At times vasians will form close attachments to particular humans but, like the ramoras, they have never been domesticated.

In a short memoir/article on the genesis of the Rockall project, Sarjeant expands on this intriguing aspect of telepathy, which for him is evidently not merely an idle fancy, and echoes, for example, some of the iconoclastic parapsychological research of scientist Rupert Sheldrake:

> Yes, Rockall is an imaginary place, and private fantasy, and yes, since I believe in telepathy, I utilize mental links with animals that exceed any real-world parallels (though always careful to confine the mental interplay within the probable capacities of those beasts). Moreover, my invented animals and plants are all perfectly possible survivals of, or descendants from, creatures known from fossil remains in Tertiary strata.[9]

In the same memoir, Sarjeant also speculates on how one might classify his fiction: "All in all, my novels fall somewhere in the hinterland between science fiction, science fantasy and historical fiction. Rider Haggard would have called them 'romances' but alas! that useful term now has Harlequinian overtones".[10]

Written in the first person, the narrative proper of *Princes* opens in the England of 1403 immediately in the wake of the Battle of Shrewsbury as a quest story driven by filial piety. After his father and brother are defeated in this battle and are forced to flee England and the wrath of the victorious King Henry IV, young Simon Branthwaite, the protagonist, chooses to leave his native Hallamshire and seek them in the semilegendary realm of Lyonesse, somewhere to the west of England in Rockall. In the port city of Bristol, Simon makes friends with Avran, whose life he saves from assassins. Avran is a prince and a member of the family that rules the realm of Sandastre at the southern end of Rockall. The two board a ship in Bristol and make landfall in Sandarro, the capital of Sandastre, and there Simon, as a master archer, becomes an instructor to the Sandastrian military and an honored guest and citizen of the country. At the same time, he falls in love with Ilven, Avran's sister, a Sandastrian princess, but their betrothal is postponed by Simon's unbending need to pursue his search for his father and brother.

Together, enjoying a succession of episodes of high adventure, Simon and Avran travel north through Rockall's several realms in a richly various landscape, one that bears the stamp of a broad cultural, anthropological, botanical, and biological diversity. In the fourth book of the series, Simon is reunited with his father and brother in Lyonesse, a place that has been closely connected with Arthurian legend. From there, Simon and Avran wend their way back south again and become involved in the politics and power struggles of the principalities that lie between them and Sandarro. Some of these principalities have an ethnic and cultural resonance with Britain and Europe. For example, there is a kingdom, Mionia, founded by settlers from Ireland. There is also a place that has become a refuge for remnant elements of the Knights Templar, fugitives without a base or homeland after the dissolution of their order. The quartet of novels that follows the initial four novels ends with the capture and enslavement of Simon by the Mentonese.

The concluding quartet of novels introduces a new first-person narrator, namely, Caradoc, a young Welshman who finds his way into Rockall after having been lost at sea on a fishing trip. He too becomes a slave of the Mentonese and joins forces with Simon. Together, they escape and meet up with Avran. The three of them make their way to Sandastre to warn of an impending invasion by the resurgent Vragansaratans – the oppressive people who had once held sway over most of Rockall but were vanquished in the wake of the natural cataclysm that overwhelmed the original Atlantis-like landmass. In the climactic ending, with their help, the would-be conquerors are overcome, and Simon is reunited with Ilven.

There are creative elaborations that I, as editor and rewriter, want to work into a larger conception of the series as a whole that quite excite me. As a mythical place with real-world resonances in the historically vibrant area of the North Atlantic, Rockall serves as an ideal catchment for a number of themes that I feel would contribute to a richer narrative fabric and that could be woven into the story arc as the series unfolds in subsequent novels, which remain a work in progress at this stage. To speak in metaphorical terms, I regard Bill Sarjeant's world of Rockall as a kind of fruitfully generative rootstock tree, capable of absorbing a wide variety of graftings. One of these, for example, is the rich mother lode of Arthurian legends, which Sarjeant does indeed make allusion to, but which could easily be amplified. In particular, the final resting place of Arthur is heavily laden with mystery and controversy, as are the time and place of his flourishing, not to mention his very historicity. Other themes for possible exploration and elaborations include the Robin Hood legends and historical events such as the Peasants' Revolt of 1381 under the leadership of Wat Tyler.

In its early 15th century manifestation, Rockall is a large and, in many ways, unexplored continent with room for colonization by different peoples. The possibility of weaving other ethnological themes into the longer narrative also attracts me as a means of conveying a sense of mutual connection and interpenetration with the history of our own world, especially given Rockall's geographical placement.[11]

For example, there are the far-roving Vikings that could be introduced into this large and expansive canvas of story. I'm thinking, too, of colonists from Roman Britain, the late stages of which remain something of an evocatively mysterious realm to scholars. There are other possibilities as well. One that intrigues me arises from a controversial book by an Italian scholar, Felice Vinci, who speculates that the ancient Greeks and the Homeric epics originated in the Baltic area, which would be a relatively near neighbor of Rockall in the North Atlantic. He proposes that the ancient Greeks migrated south from the Baltic to the mainland of present-day Greece at a time of climate change, bringing with them their tales and legends, which became the basis for *The Iliad* and *The Odyssey*.[12] Yet another theme that piques my interest and that could be introduced into Rockall arises from the interesting work of Boston University geology professor Robert Schoch in the area of alternative archaeology – a field of study that provides endlessly fertile ground for the subcreation of alternative worlds. In his book *Voyages of the Pyramid Builders* (2001), Schoch speculates, for example, that there was a proto-civilization of pyramid-building people who were driven out of their homeland, this being a variation on what cultural anthropologists call the diffusionist theory of civilization.[13]

Underlying the story of Rockall, of course, as its legendary matrix in deep time, is the story of Atlantis, with Sarjeant postulating Rockall to be a geological remnant of the catastrophic inundation of that much-mooted civilization.

An only child, Sarjeant was born on July 15, 1935, in Sheffield, England, St. Swithin's Day; St. Swithin having been an Anglo-Saxon bishop of Winchester. Hence, one presumes, his middle name, which he adopted for his pen name as a novelist, Antony Swithin, to distinguish his fiction from his other voluminous writings. His father, Harold Sarjeant, was a storekeeper, and his mother, Margaret, was a legal assistant. Both of Sarjeant's parents were keenly interested in archaeology, which served as a stimulus to his own interest in the past. As he explains in a short memoir/article on the genesis of the Rockall project, Sarjeant fell victim as a child to successive illnesses.[14] That and not having siblings forced him to depend on his own devices for amusement and intellectual stimulation. At the age of five, in 1940, he was in hospital for a tonsillectomy when a German bombing raid caused him to be moved hastily to an air-raid shelter, where he came very close to dying. In a short but fascinating memoir, he talks about being moved to a hospital annex for the dying, the youngest patient there, and recalls the coffin trolleys coming and going with the deceased. His being sent home, he continues, coincided with the "blitz", the greatest bombing raid on Sheffield, which witnessed the destruction of the whole city center, with many hundreds of people being killed or injured. It was a night lit by burning buildings and loud with the "pow-pow" of Junkers' bomber engines, a night that he spent with neighbors, since both his parents were air-raid wardens. In his convalescence, he was sent to a small private school run by two elderly sisters. He notes his early years as having been an essentially solitary existence, days spent reading, looking at or drawing maps, and, as he says, affording him time to "build in my mind my own imaginary world". Books, however, were few in those straitened wartime circumstances. Nonetheless, like his mother, Sarjeant became a great fan of H. Rider Haggard, whose *King Solomon's Mines* (1885) he read with deep fascination, which led him to seek out his other novels. He also became enthralled by Edgar Rice Burroughs, particularly *The Gods of Mars* (1913), *The Warlord of Mars* (1913–1914), *The Son of Tarzan* (1915–1916), and *Jungle Girl* (1932), all of which were to be found on his parents' bookshelves. The broadcast readings of Lord Dunsany's stories also shaped and fascinated his inchoate imaginative life.

However, Sarjeant notes, it was atlas maps that truly fired his imagination and propelled him into the world of Rockall, which became almost more real to him than England. He speculates, in fact, that his interest in geology may have been sparked by the very name of this alternative world, as he had already conceived the desire to become a geologist and was taking delight in finding fossil plants in the back garden amid the rubble from air-raid shelter excavations.

He mentions too that Philip Woodruff's *The Sword of Northumbria* (1948), a historical romance-cum-fantasy now long out of print, became a seminal influence. Indeed, in later years, not only did he write a review essay in praise of the latter, urging its republication, but he corresponded with Woodruff, the pen name of Philip Mason, a versatile, multifaceted British civil servant who wrote a number of books, including a two-volume work on the British Raj. A further, exceedingly vivid impression was made on Sarjeant by the radio version of Conan Doyle's *The Lost World* (1912). Unsurprisingly, he was to become a Conan Doyle aficionado and Sherlock Holmes scholar, explaining in one of his many divagations into the realm of literature, which were often linked to his academic expertise as a geologist, that it was Conan Doyle's keen interest in a fossil track discovery on his own property that prompted the writing of *The Lost World*.[15]

My own sense is that *The Lost World* provided a kind of rough template and spur to Sarjeant's imagination. H. Greenhough Smith, editor of *The Strand Magazine* (1891–1950), where many of the Sherlock Holmes stories were published and where, in 1912, *The Lost World* was serialized, recounts the impetus that drove Conan Doyle's creation of this novel. It began as a wager. Apparently, a friend of Conan Doyle's had contended that the possibilities for a new type of action-adventure story

> had been exhausted and that with the pirate ship, the treasure hunt, and the other well-known forms of adventure books no new thrill was possible. The novelist, on the contrary, upheld the view that there was a large field which had not yet been worked, and that it should develop upon the lines of a combination of imagination and realism each pushed as far as the writer's capacity would carry him. The argument ended in a small bet and a promise by Sir Arthur that he would endeavour to vindicate his opinion by producing such a book. The result is *The Lost World*.[16]

Also, in one of his letters to editor Smith, Conan Doyle makes a pointed allusion to world-building and the high premium he placed on it: "I think it will make the very best serial . . . that I have ever done, especially when it has its trimming of fake photos, maps, and plans".[17]

A tall, solidly built Yorkshireman, Sarjeant enrolled as an undergraduate at the University of Sheffield, where he obtained his BSc in geology in 1956. After this, still at the University of Sheffield, he embarked on his PhD. His explanation for coming to choose Jurassic dinoflagellates, which are prehistoric marine microfossils, as his thesis topic as against other alternatives illustrates nicely the imaginative cast of his mind. He suggests, in fact, that the word "dinoflagellate" may have swayed him toward this choice, inasmuch as it was, as he terms it, "a beguiling echo of the word 'dinosaur'". In the course of these studies, in demonstration of the impressive range of his intellect, avid poet that he was, he succeeded in carrying off the University poetry prize. At the same time, he indulged in what were to be lifelong interests – that is, haunting secondhand bookshops and playing and singing folk music, as well as photography. In 1963, he took a position as assistant lecturer at the University of Nottingham. In 1967–1968, he was appointed a visiting professor at the University of Oklahoma at Norman, which served as an introduction to life in North America. This led in turn to his acceptance of a position in Canada in 1972 as a professor of geology at the University of Saskatchewan in Saskatoon, where he was to remain for the next 30 years until his death.

During all these years, his scholarly output was prodigiously enormous, running to 275 publications. Besides his expertise in dinoflagellates, Sarjeant also became a major figure in the study of the fossil trackways of dinosaurs and their fellow vertebrates, as well as the history of geology. Among his major achievements was a stupendously massive ten-volume bibliography, *Geologists and the History of Geology* (1978–1993), which ran to over 8,000 pages and for which he was awarded several honors. Also, he wrote one of the first textbooks on marine microfossils, *Fossil and Living Dinoflagellates* (1974), as well as coauthoring a major study of dinosaur footprints, *The Tracks of Triassic Vertebrates* (1997), with Geoffrey Tresise. During the last two years of his life, in a further demonstration of the breadth of his scholarly curiosity, Sarjeant evinced an interest in paleontological and geological folklore and was contemplating a more ample treatment of the prehistoric origins of mythical creatures, like the dragon and the cyclops, for example. By the end of his life, his book collection ran to an astonishing 85,000 volumes, mostly in geology, but also including works of mystery fiction, fantasy, humor, children's books, music, and travel.

In Saskatoon, he helped to found a local folk music group, "The Prairie Higglers", with whom he played English and other folk songs for more than 20 years. From 1979 to 1980, he was president of the Saskatoon Nature Society, while from 1986 to 1989 he was president of the Canadian Folk Music Society. He was also closely involved during this time in local history and heritage ventures. Sarjeant has been succinctly described as having had a "down-to-earth nature and complete lack of any superficial airs". Meanwhile, his colleague, French palae-ontologist Philippe Taquet, recalls him as being "a marvelous companion, full of humour, a love of life and amusing stories, with an encyclopedic knowledge of the history of geology and palaeontology, whose knowledge and culture extended to many other subjects . . . to travel in his company and to listen to his stories was a source of joy and discovery".[18]

It is vitally important to properly contextualize Bill Sarjeant's achievement within the broader sweep of English literature and intellectual history. We live in a time of high mutability, of modernity and postmodernity *à l'outrance*, when so many of the age-old verities, shared as a common heritage across many cultures, have been swept away as by a tsunami, sundering us from what C. S. Lewis called the Tao, "which others may call Natural Law or Traditional Morality or the First Principles of Natural Reason or the First Platitudes . . . the sole source of all value judgments".[19]

Fallen victim as well to this seismic cultural dislocation is the "doctrine of virtue", a cross-cultural concept, cognate to the Tao, that stretches back to Plato and beyond and that philosopher Josef Pieper calls "one of the great discoveries in the history of man's self-understanding".[20] Indeed, the four commonly referenced virtues – prudence, fortitude, justice, temperance – are called "cardinal" from the Latin word for "hinge". While the idea of virtue as a hinge has receded and has become a quaint outpost in our cultural memory, it is nonetheless undergoing the stirrings of a revival. I am thinking here of the momentous intellectual éclat of a book like *After Virtue* (1981), Alasdair MacIntyre's landmark defense of the moral necessity of returning to a classical Aristotelian understanding of this concept, this "discarded image" – to borrow a metaphor from C. S. Lewis – one that predates the upheavals of modernity.

In an interview he gave in 1991 to *Green and White*, the University of Saskatch-ewan alumni magazine, Sarjeant, sensing the gap between his own sensibilities, forged as they were in an older world – he had vivid memories of his childhood during the height of the Battle of Britain – and that of other contemporary writ-ers, remarked mordantly that in fantasy "at the moment so many writers are so depressing, so *black*! . . . I can't read that. It may be a very pessimistic generation. I think it probably is. But it's just a thing I don't share".[21]

If one were looking for a shorthand description of the larger significance of Bill Sarjeant and his work, it would not be inappropriate to confer on him honorary status *in absentia* as one of the last of the Inklings, that Oxford group of writers and intellectuals, most illustrious for its inclusion of Tolkien and Lewis in their number, who "by returning to the fundamentals of story and explor-ing its relation to faith, virtue, self-transcendence, and hope, have renewed a current that runs through the heart of Western literature, beginning with Virgil and the *Beowulf* poet: that they have recovered archaic literary forms not as an antiquarian curiosity but as a means of squarely addressing modern anxieties and longings".[22]

In his penetratingly eloquent review of Tolkien's *Fellowship of the Ring*, C. S. Lewis describes the work as being "like lightning from a clear sky", a dramatically innovative achievement that belongs to a history of heroic romance that stretches back to *The Odyssey*, one that has appeared, however, "at a period almost pathological in its anti-romanticism". *The Perilous Quest for Lyonesse* falls into this age-old category of heroic romance in a world that today bears an even more visceral antipathy to such a worldview than was the case in Lewis's time. Meanwhile, within this romantic framework, it boasts its own, altogether unique, compass and imaginative vision. Bill Sarjeant was a scholar of world renown, a man anchored in the perspective of long temporal vistas that arose, in his case, from his academic discipline of geology. Just as philology was the *idée maîtresse* for Tolkien, far from being merely an earthbound science, geology was for Sarjeant a bridge into a realm of fecund imagining, a springboard into the world of Rockall, which he had begun building in his childhood. Sarjeant, I believe, was an explorer in the same realm of nostalgia and drank from the same fountainhead of profound human longing as did Tolkien and also C. S. Lewis, who called this concept *sehnsucht*.

In his classic essay "On Fairy-Stories" (1939), Tolkien says that these ancient tales are noteworthy for the appeal of antiquity that they possess even more so than their beauty and horror. He speaks of them as being marked by "distance and a great abyss of time, not measurable even by *twe tusend Johr*". They serve, he explains, to satisfy "certain primordial human desires" such as the desire "to survey the depths of space and time" and the desire "to hold communion with other living things".[23] Tolkien sheds further light on this spatiotemporal aspect of faërie in one of his letters, where he attributes the attraction of *The Lord of the Rings* to "glimpses of a large history in the background: an attraction like that of viewing far off an unvisited island, or seeing the towers of a distant city gleaming in a sunset mist".[24] Mirroring this insight, Sarjeant transposes his sense of distance and a great abyss of time into the framework of an elaborately articulated narrative, using the quasi-historical and geological scaffolding of his alternative island world of Rockall to achieve the same evocative sense of ultimate, plangent realities that lie outside the sober, often stifling, routine of our workaday lives in an all-too-dreary sublunary world. In doing so, he builds a world that by virtue of its distinct otherness trails clouds of glory, even while retaining the characteristics of a cultural and physical landscape that is recognizable as our own. It is a subtle dialectic, and balance is achieved only with consummate wisdom and an exquisite sense of the fundamental realities of the human condition.

In its original conception, *The Perilous Quest for Lyonesse* is, as mentioned earlier, a 12-novel sequence set in the early 15th century, mostly in Rockall, an imaginary continent in the North Atlantic. Rockall is a world that in many respects rivals Tolkien's Middle-earth in its exquisitely detailed creativity, it profligate amplitude, while at the same time being incommensurably sui generis in its magic realism, organized around a framework that eschews the ill-sorted phantasmagoria that marks the countless epigones of Tolkien. It is literally a grounded world – what one might expect from a professor of geology – and manages to achieve a matchless equipoise between the real and the fantastic.

As I've noted elsewhere,[25] in the realm of fairy tale and, by extension, fantasy, a special, oftentimes sinister, significance is attributed to the in-between places, the earthen boundary between forest and ploughland, for example, or the in-between times like dawn and twilight, which mark the slow-stepping progressions of day and night toward one another. At the same time, these places and times of shape-shifting uncertainty are suggestive of mystery and hopeful possibility. In many ways, such boundaries stand as a metaphor for the dangers and ambiguities that mark the frontiers of human experience in all its enigmatic fragility, touching on abiding realities like birth and death, sickness and health, loss and gain, wayfaring and homecoming, and so on.

Similarly, in an uncanny echo of this vital aspect of our humanness, fantasy as a literary genre occupies the uncertain, frontier area between what's "true to life" and soaring flights of the imagination that beckon the reader toward the unfamiliar and the strange. For those of us who practice the craft of words, fantasy can pose some serious artistic challenges, precisely because it occupies such perilously unsure ground. Writing speculative fiction can be a tough row to hoe, as we try to negotiate our way through the pitfalls and dangers of the ground that lies between a sturdy realism and the figments conjured by our imagination. I would argue that this is an endeavor that requires not only the exercise of high standards of good judgment, but a coherent metaphysics, a system of first principles that does not collide with a willing suspension of disbelief, to use the words of Coleridge. In achieving such seamless coherence, it seems to me that Tolkien reigns as the supreme master, balancing the real against the fantastic within a metaphysical framework that is uncommonly, indeed sedulously, rigorous, as has been explicated by more than one commentator, pointing to the elaborate architectonic precision of his starkly anti-modern weltanschauung.[26] The grave risk for lesser mortals is that of falling into the realm of the arbitrarily phantasmal and a storytelling disconnected with random unevenness from reality. A distinctive mark of Sarjeant's genius is his painstaking recognition of this axiomatic need to avoid any diminution of the illusion of the reality of his alternative world, a world cognate with our own, but alluringly different. It is worthwhile to remember here the etymology of the word "illusion", which comes from the Latin *in-ludere*, "to be in play", which in turn suggests a timeless stepping outside of the diurnal round of life. Romantic rationalist that he was, Sarjeant pursued a fairly strict exclusion of plot devices that depend on the miraculous and hence added plausibility to his portrayal of Rockall. This is not to say, however, that he does not have thematic elements that are arrestingly strange, evocatively suggestive.

With Sarjeant, there are a number of metaphysical points of departure that undergird his work and facilitate an invitation to the reader to enter his alternative world. For one, his work demonstrates an instinctive appreciation for a concept that is richly exemplified in the Middle Ages, that of *analogia entis*, "analogy of being", which has been described as a "method of predication whereby concepts derived from a familiar object are made applicable to a relatively unknown object in virtue of some similarity between two otherwise dissimilar objects".[27] This is not an abstrusely otiose observation. There are some who see the rejection of an analogical understanding of reality by medieval nominalists like William of Ockham and Duns Scotus as having laid the inchoate groundwork of the modern world – a momentous epistemological sea change that led directly to Cartesian rationalism and a subsequently disenchanted world, bereft of truth, goodness, and beauty – that is, what we call the transcendentals. The grave ramifications of this disenchantment were perceived acutely in the 19th century by a thinker like Nietzsche, who recognized it as a yawning abyss and civilizational crisis, the only possible response to which he saw as a nihilistic calculus revolving around the will to power. In its wake came the loss of a sense of beauty as a value and a goal in literature and the arts.

These days, in a general cultural climate of grotesque desecration and a headlong flight from enchantment, beauty has been relegated to moldering obscurity and is a criterial standard that is seldom invoked as an end in itself. In early draft notes for his essay "On Fairy-Stories", however, with an iconoclastic disregard for the fashionable austerity and ugliness of modernism, Tolkien defines faërie as "the power to achieve beauty", which he calls "a magic related to the mystery of art".[28] He explains, moreover, that it is an ideal "state wherein will[,] imagination and desire are directly effective – within the limitations of the world. Above all where beauty – of all three the most magical – is natural and relatively effortless".[29] In other words, beauty is for Tolkien a liberating transcendental inextricably conjoined with the good and true. Critic Michael Milburn cross-references Tolkien's conception of faërie as related to beauty and imagination with the approach of Coleridge, for whom the imagination was closely aligned with his exquisite sensitivity to nature and described in his "Dejection: An Ode" as "this beautiful and beauty-making power".[30] This acute sense of Coleridge's can be felt as well with a stark, mighty, almost palpably overpowering force in a poem like *Hymn Before Sun-rise, in the Vale of Chamouni*. For Tolkien, as for Coleridge, beauty is an objective reality outside of the self, not simply just a subjective reaction.[31] Also, with Tolkien and with Sarjeant, no less than with Coleridge, beauty achieves a particularly vivid manifestation in landscape, which is inevitably implicated in world-building. Hence, it would not be unfair to say that world-building is a uniquely appropriate vehicle for the expression of beauty. I am reminded here of the evocative effect a classic book like *The Making of the English Landscape* (1955) by W. G. Hoskins had on poet W. H. Auden, who was, of course, an unstinting admirer of Tolkien's achievement.[32]

To the diagnosis of Nietzsche, Alasdair MacIntyre posits as his own response a return to an Aristotelian teleology and sees virtue as best conveyed through story. This accords with Aristotle's *Poetics*, where Aristotle gives story a place of primacy over and above other elements of literary art.[33] Elsewhere, in his *Metaphysics*,

Aristotle notes that "the lover of myth or story (*philomuthai*) . . . is in a sense a philosopher".[34] Stories mediate to us our worldview, our philosophical conclusions about life. Like life itself, stories are inherently linear and teleological, with episodic, picaresque narrative being the exception rather than the rule. Critic Northrop Frye describes the essential element of plot in romance as adventure, "which means that romance is naturally a sequential and processional form. . . . The complete form of the romance is clearly the successful quest, and such a completed form has three main stages: the stage of the perilous journey and the preliminary minor adventures; the crucial struggle . . . and the exaltation of the hero".[35] Jung placed such a high premium on romantic narrative precisely because it acts as a kind of unalloyed distillate of story, lending itself more readily than other forms to the mythical resonances of the hero's journey, with whose typology the Rockall series overlaps in no small part.[36] A metaphysics of transcendence is woven into the very fabric of such a journey, which by its very nature resists nihilism and desacralization. By necessity of its form, it does not take place in a dead Cartesian wasteland, where Nietzsche raves in ironic despair like King Lear's fool, but rather in a deceptively simple but complex space between time and eternity, an atelier that is exquisitely fitted to the perennial aspects of the human condition.

No small part of Bill Sarjeant's enduring genius lies in his echoing this ancient, primordial dispensation, which survives for us as scarcely more than a faintly limned fossil track, as it were, tokening a larger, ancient, thundering reality whose stark, strange, vivid beauty we struggle to comprehend, stranded as we are within the dull, parochial confines of modernity "as on a darkling plain", to quote that famous line of Matthew Arnold. In his inaugural lecture on assuming the chair of Medieval and Renaissance Literature at Cambridge University, C. S. Lewis portrays himself as a spokesman for Old Western Culture and urges his audience to "suspend most of the responses and unlearn most of the habits you have acquired in reading modern literature". He ends with a fanciful but incisive metaphor, describing himself as a specimen of a bygone age and postulates with more than a hint of sere, autumnal melancholy that "there are not going to be many more dinosaurs".[37] Alas, Lewis spoke truth, even while allowing for the possibility of unexpected survivals. The brilliantly achieved conjunction of tradition and originality that invests the timeless world of Rockall is indeed such a survival, a bridgehead of light in a world bereft of the transcendent. It is what makes Bill Sarjeant's work one of those splendid exceptions that proves the rule, a dinosaurian specimen that lives and endures, now cleaned and burnished, well worth fostering in its profoundly merited phase of resurrection.

Notes

1. C. J. Jung, *Spirit in Man, Art, and Literature*, translators R. F. C. Hull, Princeton: Princeton University Press, 1971, pp. 115, 120.
2. Ovid, *Ars Amatoria*, "Liber Secundus", line 313, available at www.perseus.tufts.edu/hopper/text?doc=Perseus%3Atext%3A1999.02.0068%3Atext%3DArs%3Abook%3D2

3. Jacob Bronowski, *The Ascent of Man*, n.p.: BBC Books, 2011, p. 388.
4. Antony Swithin, "Tolkien – and Swithin – Beneath the North Atlantic Ocean", *Beyond Bree*, April, 2001.
5. William Antony Swithin Sarjeant, "The Geology of Middle-earth", in Patricia Reynolds and Glen GoodKnight, editors, *Proceedings of the J.R.R. Tolkien Centenary Conference, Keble College, Oxford, 1992*, Milton Keynes and Altadena: The Tolkien Society, 1995, pp. 334–339.
6. William A. S. Sarjeant, "The Shire: Its Bounds, Food and Farming", *Mallorn*, September, 2001, Vol. 39, pp. 33–37.
7. For an in-depth discussion of this theme, cf. Michael Alexander, *Medievalism: The Middle Ages in Modern England*, Yale and New Haven: Yale University Press, 2017.
8. Antony Swithin, *Princes of Sandastre*, London: Fontana/Collins, 1990.
9. William A. S. Sarjeant, "Shaping an Imaginary World: The Genesis of the Rockall Stories", in J. Webb and A. Enstice, editors, *The Fantastic Self*, North Perth, Australia: Eidolon Publications, 1999, pp. 19–27.
10. Ibid.
11. Cf. Michael Pye, *The Edge of the World: How the North Sea Made Us Who We Are*, New York: Viking, 2014.
12. Felice Vinci, *The Baltic Origins of Homer's Epic Tales*, Rochester, VT: Inner Traditions, 2005.
13. Robert Schoch, *Voyages of the Pyramid Builders,* New York: Tarcher/Penguin, 2003.
14. Op. cit.; William A. S. Sarjeant, "Shaping an Imaginary World: The Genesis of the Rockall Stories", p. 19.
15. R. Dana Batory and William A.S. Sarjeant, "Sussex *Iguanodon* Footprints and the Writing of *The Lost World*", in David D. Gillette and Martin G. Lockley, editors, *Dinosaur Tracks and Traces*, Cambridge: Cambridge University Press, 1989, pp. 13–18.
16. H. G. Smith, "Some Letters of Sir Arthur Conan Doyle", *Strand* Magazine, October, 1930, p. 395
17. John Dickson Carr, *The Life of Sir Arthur Conan Doyle*, London: Murray, 1949, p. 319.
18. From the obituary by Richard Howarth in *Proceedings of the Geologists' Association* 114, 367–374.
19. C. S. Lewis, *The Abolition of Man*, New York: Macmillan, 1947, p. 28.
20. Josef Pieper, *The Four Cardinal Virtues*, translators, Richard Winston, Clara Winston, Lawrence E. Lynch, and Daniel F. Coogan, New York: Harcourt Brace, 1965, p. xi.
21. "The Amazing Professor Sarjeant", *Green and White,* Spring, 1991, pp. 4–6. (*Green and White* is the alumni magazine of the University of Saskatchewan.)
22. Philip Zaleski, and Carol Zaleski, *The Fellowship: The Literary Lives of the Inklings*, New York: Farrar, Straus and Giroux, 2015, p. 512.
23. J. R. R. Tolkien, "On Fairy-Stories", *The Monsters and the Critics and Other Essays*, London: George Allen and Unwin, 1983.
24. J. R. R. Tolkien, *The Letters of J.R.R. Tolkien*, editor, Humphrey Carpenter, London: HarperCollins, Letter 333.
25. Mark Sebanc, "In Xanadu . . . Grounding the Fantastic", in Laurie Lamson, editor, *Now Write! Science Fiction, Fantasy and Horror: Speculative Genre Exercises from Today's Best Writers and Teachers*, New York: TarcherPerigee, 2014.
26. Cf. Jonathan McIntosh, *The Flame Imperishable: Tolkien, St. Thomas, and the Metaphysics of Faërie*, Kettering, OH: Angelico Press, 2017.
27. Cited by Ralph C. Wood, "Tolkien and Postmodernism", in Ralph C. Wood, editor, *Tolkien Among the Moderns*, Notre Dame, Indiana: University of Notre Dame Press, 2015, p. 343.
28. J. R. R. Tolkien, *Tolkien on Fairy-stories*, Expanded Edition, with Commentary and Notes, editors, Verlyn Flieger and Douglas A. Anderson, London: HarperCollins, 2014, p. 269.

29. Ibid., 254.

30. Michael Milburn, "Coleridge's Definition of Imagination and Tolkien's Definition of Faery", *Tolkien Studies* 7, 2010, 55–66.

31. For a masterful philosophical treatment of beauty as an objective value from a phenomenological perspective, see Dietrich von Hildebrand, *Aesthetics*, Vol. I, Steubenville, OH: Hildebrand Project, 2016, and Vol. II, Steubenville, OH: Hildebrand Press, 2018.

32. W. G. Hoskins, *The Making of the English Landscape*, with an introduction by William Boyd, Little Toller Books, 2013.

33. Aristotle, *Poetics*, 1450b, available at Perseus Digital Library Project, Tufts University: www.perseus.tufts.edu/hopper/text?doc=Perseus%3Atext%3A1999.01.0056%3Asect ion%3D1450a

34. Aristotle, *Metaphysics* 982b, pp. 12–19, available at Perseus Digital Library Project, Tufts University: www.perseus.tufts.edu/hopper/text?doc=Perseus%3Atext%3A1999.01.00 52%3Abook%3D1%3Asection%3D982b

35. Northrop Frye, *Anatomy of Criticism*, Princeton, NJ: Princeton University Press, 2000, pp. 186–187.

36. Cf. Joseph Campbell, *The Hero With a Thousand Faces*, Bollingen Series XVII, Third Edition, Novato, CA: New World Library, 2008.

37. C. S. Lewis, *"De Descriptione Temporum"*, in *Selected Literary Essays*, Cambridge: Cambridge University Press, 1969.

4

MAKING WORLDS INTO GAMES – A METHODOLOGY

Clara Fernández-Vara and Matthew Weise

Imaginary worlds are the foundation for telling stories in a variety of media – short stories, novels, comics, television shows, films, and even toys. Games, both digital and nondigital, are also part of that media landscape. Their relationship with storytelling has been contentious in the academic realm, during the dawn of game studies as a discipline.[1] In video game industry practices, the role of narrative has always been ambiguous – while some large companies still bring in writers at the end of development, as if the story was a final touch to the games, others have long accused some action-adventure games of having "cinema envy", with many titles aspiring at being interactive movies or including long cinematic scenes to tell the story of the game.

Rather than getting lost on defining the nature of storytelling in games, we want to bring the focus back to world-building as the foundation to narrative in games. Many games take place in fictional worlds; the *Elder Scrolls* series (including *The Elder Scrolls: Oblivion* (2006) and *The Elder Scrolls: Skyrim* (2011)) take place on the continent of Tamriel. Other games have gameplay that can be understood as a story, as is the case of the *Final Fantasy* game series (1987–2016), while others may be more abstract; *Tetris* (1984) is a classic example. There are games based on preexisting worlds, such as the episodic games based on *The Walking Dead* comic books (2003–), while others create their own fictional worlds, which at times give way to stories in other media. This has been the case with *Resident Evil*, which is both a long-lived game series (1996–2017) and a film saga (2002–2016). Games have become the medium where players inhabit and become part of fictional worlds in ways that other media may not have quite allowed before.

Here we propose a method for narrative game design grounded in world-building. Narrative design consists of creating game worlds that players interact with, where the interactions, goals, and systems are understood as components of a world, as we will define in more detail below. Other game designers start their designs by finding a mechanic, or a genre that they work upon, which afterward they "skin" or "theme". The focus of the game experience is on the mechanics rather than on being part of a world. Our practice differs from that of other game designers in that our games start with a fictional world or a story premise, and then we design the mechanics and seek the kinds of interactions that will allow players to interact in a world where a story unfolds as the player interacts with it.

This methodology is the result of the work of a decade, in the form of different workshops and classroom sessions. This approach has helped us and our students come up with new game interactions, rather than rehashing preexisting game conventions. Part of the innovation comes from the fact that we have encouraged people to make games out of worlds that we do not see in games enough, from the movie *Brokeback Mountain* (2005) to historical situations such as the Underground Railroad.

Narrative Design as a Discipline

What we call *narrative design* is the combination of game design and storytelling as a practice. Although it is related to writing, it is not necessarily the same thing. A game writer creates dialogue, backstory, lore, or other elements of the fictional world and the story of the game; game writing may incorporate interactive elements, such as creating dialogue choices, but creating interactions is not always part of a writer's job. On the other hand, narrative design is a form of game design that involves many subdisciplines – mechanics, systems, level, user interface, game balancing, difficulty, etc. – and applies them toward achieving a certain dramatic/emotional player experience. This discipline is not exclusively interested in other aesthetics of player experience, such as challenge, competition, achievement, or "fun" as an end in itself. The goal is to embark the player through an emotional journey, pushing them to engage with conflict in a literary sense – as opposed to a sporting sense – and helping players live through a dramatic experience.

A good way to illustrate how narrative design is a distinct discipline is the way a narrative designer would approach a design scenario. Imagine the design of a light resource-management tank combat game, where two sides attempt to destroy the other while collecting ammo, fuel, and other elements along the way. The mechanics are sound, everything seems to work, and now the designer is looking to induce a specific player experience. If the game had a skill/e-sports experiential focus, the designer would tweak the rules, variables, and other systemic properties to make it so no enemy tank was too hard or too easy to defeat, so the player never ran out of ammo or fuel but still had to work to find it. But if the game has a narrative focus, the approach would be different. For instance, the tank game could focus on the story of two siblings forced to fight on opposite sides of a civil war as tank pilots, where the player controls one of them. A narrative designer might make one sibling's tank more difficult to defeat than the rest, in order to ensure it is the final tank left, and to facilitate a dramatic climax where the player duels with the sibling. The designer also might add rules so that, if the sibling has an opportunity to fire on the player's tank, they will always hesitate; they can also add rules where, if the player lines up a shot with the sibling's tank, the sibling will shout from a loudspeaker "No! Wait!" This is all game design. It is also combat design, balancing, artificial intelligence, and resource balancing as well as writing. And it is all for the purpose of making the player feel like they are involved in a familial confrontation in the midst of a civil war. The design at all these levels is narrative design.

One of the few activities that a narrative designer does not share with other types of designers is creating and maintaining the world of the game. They may do this in conjunction with a writer or by themselves if they are the only ones in charge of the story of the game. On a large-scale project this may mean maintaining a *bible*, which is the core world-building reference document for the team. This concept is borrowed from television, where the bible is the document that tells the backstory, the characters, and the main story lines of a show; it is the referent for the writing team. In games, there is a misconception that game bibles are only the *lore*, meaning the optional backstory of the people, places, and objects; the lore is something that players can read and explore but may not be essential to play the game. A good game bible will also function as systems design reference guide, providing the context for the world's rules of cause and effect. On a properly managed story-focused game project, the world logic organically informs the game logic and vice versa.

Methodology: Worlds as Story Engines

The method described here is grounded in narrative design; we have used it in our practice and taught it in workshops all over the world. According to this method, the world of the game (either fictional or based on the real world and historical events) becomes the foundation of the game design, so the mechanics of the game deal with the themes, structures, and actions of the world itself. This does not mean that the resulting game or games are story driven – this methodology is based on abstracting core elements into game actions, elements, and systems, so the final result could be a variety of genres, from a strategy game, a role-playing game, a music game, or a puzzle game, to name but a few examples.

We look at worlds as *story engines*, where the different elements have the potential to create different stories based on the same world. Narrative *in potentia* is essential for games, since it will be players who participate in those stories, *actualizing* them if we may continue with our Aristotelian concepts. This engine is important for digital games, particularly for those designers who want to encourage emergent storytelling, but it is also useful for other genres as well as to create content for other media. We just mentioned bibles as documents which help identify the relevant parts of the story engine.

There is a long-standing assumption in the world of video games that narrative and rules are naturally opposed.[2] Players often complain about how the story got in the way of the game or vice versa, while it is also common for developers to speak of struggling to reconcile story with gameplay to make them feel coherent together. While gameplay and story are in constant friction, the difficulty mostly derives from the mental models as well as business and development practices, rather than anything inherent to the games or stories. The creative act of story and game crafting are more similar than they appear, specifically when we look at them through the lens of world-building as the foundation for both. Understanding how novelists, playwrights, screenwriters, and other media creators approach world-building is key to understanding how works in traditional media are more similar to games than generally thought.

Traditional storytellers can also approach their writing in ways that resonate with game design. J. K. Rowling explained how she prepared to write her Harry Potter series: "I spent a lot of time inventing the rules for the magical world so that I knew the limits of magic. Then I had to invent the different ways wizards could accomplish certain things".[3] Rowling sets the rules of the world and establishes what can or cannot be done, similar to how game designers define the space of possibility of their games through rules. Experienced storytellers construct story as rules, as cause and effect, as limitations that not even they can break. The story as the sequence of events in a narrative results from those rules and causal relationships playing themselves out.

Story and game may seem naturally opposed to game designers and players because what they are noticing is that story and gameplay do not always happen at the same time. The story results from world-building, and world-building includes characters, places, rules, logic, context – all set up as our story engine. Characters have motivations, desires, and goals that come into conflict with other characters or the larger systems of society they live in. Stories are bound to happen when one sets the right world elements in motion. The job of a storyteller and a narrative game designer is to select those elements so they produce the desired dramatic effect for the audience, for the players. Novelists take the rules and systems they create, run them in their imagination, and write them down in the form of a novel. Narrative game designers take the rules and systems they create and give them to other people to run and interact with them in the form of a game. Worlds are systems, and stories are one instance of the system output. Characters, environment, and relationships create the rules of the world. Tackling conflicts generates gameplay. China Miéville cites role-playing games as a major influence on his work and calls his practice "systematizing the world", just like a game designer would.[4] Novelists and game designers have the same job: creating convincing universes of cause-and-effect that feel dramatic, believable, and absorbing.

The process of creating a game from a specific world involves abstracting that world into essential elements. This process has been discussed at length in game studies[5] and is a key tool in game design. A game world (fictional or not) cannot really include all the details of the world it is based on – the Holodeck is far from being a reality. And it is not because of technological capabilities not being quite there, but rather because players need to be able to grasp how it works. The worlds of the *Grand Theft Auto* series are supposedly realistic, but they do not include getting fined for skipping a red light, while the driving mechanics often defy the actual laws of physics – and that's precisely why they are compelling. A satirical video from *The Onion*[6] explained how the next fictional installment of a first-person shooter would be "realistic" by having players haul equipment and fill out paperwork as well as spending hours looking at nothing, which would be the authentic experience of a soldier. The satire shows that first-person shooters do leave out certain aspects of warfare – such as waiting, bureaucracy, and having to go to the bathroom – while they amplify others, including killing to the extent of becoming a mass murderer. These two examples go to show that, even in supposedly realistic games using the latest technology, there are things that are left out, stylized, or exaggerated. This selection of elements is one of the things that turns game design into artistic practice, since it involves an artistic filter to interpret a world to represent it. One could also design a game like the one proposed by *The Onion*, where all the player does is carry equipment and fill out paperwork – it would be a different abstraction of the same world, and it would also be a completely different statement about what it means to be a soldier on the battlefield.

Another advantage to designing games by thinking about the world first is that it is a better approach to introduce people from outside game design to the creation of games – fictional worlds are a concept that is more familiar than systems design. We have taught this workshop to educators, musical theater writers, composers, filmmakers, and marketers, to name but a few. This game design methodology can facilitate attracting more diverse people into game design, since the focus is not on systems design or its relationship with math or computer science – both disciplines already struggle to attract diversity – but on world-building.

This world-driven game design method focuses on two aspects in order to set up what aspects of the world will be abstracted: a breakdown of the conflicts of the world and a list of actions – in the form of verbs – that define what can happen in the world. What these two aspects are, their origins, and how they work, will be discussed in the following sections.

Conflict

Drama is often associated with conflict, since dramatic action is often driven by trying to solve conflict. It is a key element in screenwriting manuals and a way of understanding story that seems quite common in Hollywood screenwriting.

The relevance of conflict in game design does not come from believing that games are competitions; Caillois talks about *agon* as one type of game among others.[7] Rather, the approach to conflict for us comes from thinking about gameplay as dramatic action and relating games to theater (something that Caillois also does in his classification). While writing a paper on using Stanislavski's method acting applied to game design, we examined how he proposes that actors should identify the motivations of a character, which started by identifying what their objectives are:

> Stanislavski argued that in order to transform a performance into something "interesting to watch" every objective must have a conflict associated to it. The conflict opposes the objective. Usually, conflict arises from two opposite objectives. Characters try to end the conflict to achieve their objectives through actions. Therefore, conflicts generate actions performed to end those conflicts. . . . The clash between the objective and the conflict is what makes a performance into something that gains the audience's attention.[8]

Therefore, dramatic action derives from how characters try to achieve their goals. What was illuminating in this case is the three types of conflicts that Stanislavski provided for actors: intersubjective, environmental, and intimate. Intersubjective conflict happens between characters who have opposite objectives; environmental conflicts arise from the world the character is in, interfering with achieving the objective; intimate conflicts are those where the actions of the character bring about internal consequences. This classification of conflicts provided a road map for the different levels in which characters can tackle a fictional world; based on this previous work, they are also good indicators of how players can enter and be in conflict with the world of a game, as discussed in that paper. Stanislavski's levels of conflict made it obvious that any fictional world is going to have a multiplicity of conflicts, based on the environment, the characters, and the relationships with each other. It is the synergies between these conflicts that will create dramatic energy that will power the story engine we are setting up as world-builders.

In applying Stanislavski's classification to world-building and game design, we realized that we needed to break down environmental conflict into the different ways in which the world could create conflict for the characters, since these different conflicts also bring about different game design approaches. Thus, environmental conflict was divided into environmental, sociocultural/economic, and informational conflict; we re-termed intersubjective conflict and intimate conflict as interpersonal and personal conflict. What follows is our own classification of conflicts in relation to world-building.

Environmental Conflict

The world is hostile to its inhabitants or visitors, so being in the space itself and surviving is a challenge. This is often referred to as "man versus nature", although the way we define environmental conflict goes beyond natural causes or doesn't have to apply to men exclusively.

Urban environments can be challenging to story protagonists, especially large cities, as is the case of London in many of the novels of Charles Dickens. We can go beyond natural and urban challenges to create pressure on the characters – a ship traveling from one point to another needs to manage its resources and cannot get external help. The challenge can be being in the middle of the ocean, as in the films *Dead Calm* (1989) or *Master and Commander: The Far Side of the World* (2003) or traveling through space, as in the TV show *Battlestar Galactica* (2004–2009). Postapocalyptic worlds are also typical examples of hostile worlds, such as the desert landscapes of the *Mad Max* saga (1979–2015), where the land is barren, and the fuel to move from one place to another is a precious resource. The world of *Blade Runner* (1982) is also postapocalyptic; although not very obvious in Ridley Scott's version, its source *Do Androids Dream of Electric Sheep?* (1968) explains that only those who have not been damaged by radiation can leave Earth. The sequel *Blade Runner 2049* (2017) makes this evident by showing the ravaged deserts around Los Angeles as well as an abandoned and half-buried Las Vegas. Plagues, including zombie apocalypses, are also examples of hostile environments, since the appearance of an illness whose remedy is not known not only makes large parts of the population sick and die but also halts the social order of the world, as we will see later.

Environmental conflict is a favorite of video game designers, since in order to tackle it, players need to manage their resources, figure out how to navigate the space, and survive by figuring out how the new unfamiliar space works, as we can see by traversing London after a zombie outbreak in *ZombiU* (2012) or the postapocalyptic landscapes of the *Fallout* series (1997–2018).

Sociocultural/Economic Conflict

This type consists of a variety of conflicts, and the one thing in common is that they pitch large groups of people against each other. These conflicts can take many shapes – social classes pitted against each other, separate economic groups, religious beliefs, ethnic and racial divisions, and different cultures and languages. Many of these conflicts relate to each other; for example, systemic oppression can keep certain ethnicities in the lower economic tiers. Sociocultural conflicts are often represented in a Manichean manner, where there are only two factions fighting each other, often following a pattern of good vs. evil (see, for example, the Jedi vs. Sith factions of *Star Wars*). This type of conflict also gives way to another narrative trope, the "fish out of water", where we find someone from one culture moving to a new place and having to learn how to live with people different from them. This is often played for comedy, but it can also be the core of a more serious story, though in this latter case it can also derive into white savior tropes, where the stranger is transformed by the new environment but ultimately comes to help a certain ethnic group in their own struggles, as seen in films such as *Dances With Wolves* (1990), *The Last Samurai* (2003), or *Avatar* (2009).

Video games resort to this kind of conflict often, as it helps in defining groups opposing each other, from the different species of *Starcraft* (1998) to the factions of *Dungeons & Dragons* (1974). These divisions help differentiating who is on the player's side or not, but the way they are treated is more like a sports team rather than providing sociocultural or economic motivations for players to feel like they belong to a group.

Informational Conflict

Not all challenges have to involve the world itself or other people, but rather, how much we know, what information is available, or what is true or not. Informational conflict accounts for how the world can tease its inhabitants (as well as the audience) on their knowledge – mystery stories thrive on informational conflict, where detectives try to figure out what has happened. Conspiracy theories can also create diverging ways of understanding the world, especially when it comes to revealing secret realities – think of the *X-Files* (1995–2002) motto, "The truth is out there". Warped, unstable, dreamlike worlds also have informational conflicts at their core, such as Philip K. Dick's novel *Ubik* (1969), the film *Inception* (2010), or the twisted mind representations of the TV show *Legion* (2017–2019). Not knowing what is real or not creates a sense of instability as well as challenges audiences to understand what the rules of the fictional world may be.

Hidden information is a basic element of game design; card games usually require players to hide their hand and challenge them to infer what others may have based their decisions on. Detective games thrive on informational conflicts, inherited from the mystery fiction genre in novels and fiction. In *Her Story* (2015), the player needs to find the video clips from a police testimony and interpret what happened, whereas in *The Return of the Obra Dinn* (2018), the player has a mechanical device to figure out how each crew member and passenger of a ship died.

Interpersonal Conflict

Part of what makes a story compelling can be to see how people clash with each other and how they resolve their differences – or not. Interpersonal conflicts can be a reflection of the groups and factions of the world, so the relationships between the characters are a synecdoche of the larger conflicts represented in the sociocultural and economic conflicts described previously. Conflicts do not always have to be adversarial – the struggle of two lovers to get together can give way to both tragedy (think of Romeo and Juliet) or comedic (see Hollywood romantic comedies of the 1990s) depending on whether the protagonists figure out their differences or not.

Games classified as *agon* create an interpersonal conflict, a rivalry, but which usually lies outside the game. In order to make this conflict personal, players need to identify with a character as well as understand other characters (whether controlled by players or not) as entities rather than tokens, something that role-playing games may be better suited to do. Live-action role-playing games (LARPs) precisely encourage the connection between players and their characters in order to make interpersonal conflicts vivid and personal to the players. On the other hand, this is difficult to achieve in digital games, where the relationship with the character is more a prosthesis than inhabiting a role.[9]

Personal Conflict

Last but not least, one's worst enemy can be oneself. Self-doubt, identity crises, or illness can cause characters to struggle on a day-to-day basis, let alone when facing all the larger conflicts already listed. Growing up is also a common way to challenge a protagonist – the genre of the bildungsroman revolves around the formation and education of a protagonist into adulthood.

Games do not challenge players at an intimate level often enough, though; the tendency of digital games to make players feel empowered and in control is not particularly compatible with personal dilemmas. There are some notable excep-tions – *The Walking Dead* adventure games (2012–2019) challenged their players to make life-and-death decisions in a matter of seconds while zombies attack, and they could see the consequences of their decisions through the story. *Papers, Please* (2013) puts the player in the role of a border agent who decides the fate of people try-ing to enter the fictional country of Arstotzka, making the players decide whether they want to be a border agent doing things by the book for little pay, behaving humanely, or taking a bribe every now and then in order to sustain one's family.

All the conflicts just listed relate to each other, where one key conflict will generate other kinds of conflicts. For example, war can start as a sociocultural/economic conflict, which then creates an environmental conflict, as it becomes difficult to travel and resources become scarcer. War also divides neighbors, friends, and families, creating the kinds of rifts that we identify with interpersonal conflict as well as being the cause of stress and trauma for the people involved in it, given that they live in a constant state of threat and have to cope with personal loss and grief on a daily basis.

One of our favorite examples of how a world can incorporate all these conflicts and create a story engine is the TV show *Battlestar Galactica* (2004–2009). TV shows are great examples of how to set up a world for potential stories; *Battlestar Galactica* describes all its conflicts in its pitch document.[10] These are some selected conflicts:

- Environmental conflict

  - Humanity has been decimated after an interplanetary nuclear attack. The last of the human race survives in the ships that were in outer space and only have the resources available to them in the ships themselves.
  - Humanity is looking for the location of the legendary planet Kobol where they may be able to settle and grow the population.

- Sociocultural/economic conflict

  - There are two main factions, the humans and the Cylons. The Cylons are robotic creations who became self-aware and rebelled against their creators, to the point of provoking the apocalypse as revenge.
  - Among the human survivors, the power of decision-making is a tug-of-war between the politicians, the military, and scientists as well as religious leaders, who want to face the Cylons and save humanity in different ways.
  - Humans come from 12 different colonies and have different beliefs and religions. Each colony has a different attitude toward the prophecies that presumably foretell how humanity will be saved.

- Informational conflict

  - At the beginning of the show, Cylons are indistinguishable from humans, which allows them to infiltrate and destroy most of humanity.
  - Humans know that Kobol may be the place that they are looking for, but they do not know where it is or whether it is real.

- Interpersonal conflict

  - The conflict between the military and the politicians is embodied in the conflict between Admiral William Adama, commander of the Battlestar Galactica, and Laura Roslin, president of the Twelve Colonies, as the highest-ranking surviving member of the presidential board. To make things more complicated, they eventually develop feelings for each other.
  - Characters are also in conflict with each other through personal relationships. For example, Admiral Adama has a tense relationship with his son Lee, also a pilot, after the death of Adama's other son Zak. Lee is also attracted to Zak's fiancée, Kara "Starbuck" Thrace, but both feel guilty about the death of Zak. After the destruction of the Twelve Colonies, the three of them have to work together.

- Personal conflict

  - Some Cylons do not know that they are Cylons until they are awoken, so they behave believing they are human. One recurring conflict is characters discovering whether they are Cylons.
  - Dreams and visions are also recurrent among characters, so several characters struggle with figuring out what is real or what is the product of their imagination, a religious epiphany, or a hallucination.

These conflicts set up the engine for the stories that unfold in each episode of the show; each episode focuses on a couple of main conflicts at a time. This same engine is also the basis of novels, comics, and games, since it identifies the sources of friction that the dramatic action can tackle and try to resolve.

In order to transform the fictional world of our choice into a story engine, our proposed method imitates Stanislavski's in applying these types to understand the fictional world of the game so we can identify the sources of tension of the world. In the same way that Stanislavski proposed that dramatic action is what will help actors and their characters solve the conflicts of a play, the gameplay will be used to tackle the conflicts of the game world. This takes us to the second part of our methodology – we have a world; now we need to devise the game mechanics that players will use to interact with it.

Verbs

In order to identify the actions that are available for the player to interact with, our method focuses on listing and examining *verbs*, as another point in common between dramatic action and game design. Why verbs? First, it is a known grammatical concept, and one doesn't need to be a game designer to understand what they are, which makes them an excellent point of overlap between interactive and traditional arts. Second, verbs are an underused game design tool, even though they have a long history both in a creative and analytical sense of being used in game design practice – verbs can be part of the process of abstraction into a game. Nintendo game designer Shigeru Miyamoto described verbs as a starting point for game design, citing the original *Super Mario Bros.* (1985) as a design experiment based entirely around how you make a single verb – *jump* – fun. Game designer and industry critic Chris Crawford also invoked verbs as a way to criticize mainstream video games, saying they don't have enough verbs.[11] If we want to push games beyond running, jumping, and shooting, the verbs that define gameplay – not just what is shown in cutscenes – must seek more variety; otherwise, somber music, morally conflicted writing, and good acting mean nothing. The verbs of a game, what the player actually does, is what a game is about, beyond what is on the blurb description of the game.

For Crawford, abstracting gameplay as a list of verbs is a way to cut through the haze of rhetoric and presentation to get right to the core of player action and thus the heart of any interactive experience. Video games can have the richness and diversity of narrative content that is lauded in film and television if their verbs, rather than just their presentation, reflect that. For Miyamoto, verbs are the starting point for game design. So why not use Miyamoto's method to address Crawford's problem? If games fall short by comparison to other traditional storytelling media, why not start with verbs? What verbs do video games avoid that we can find in other stories? Why do they avoid them? Can one list the "verb inventory" of a great story, rich in complexity and human experience? Can we use those verbs as the basis for a game? Wouldn't that be a more interesting way to adapt a film into a game than looking for the parts of the story that already have running, driving, or shooting and making the rest cutscenes?

To demonstrate how verbs function as part of the process of abstraction of a world, we will use a story world that may be familiar to many. The world of James Bond might not be what one thinks of as a great, complex story about the human experience, but it is a productive case study. First, there are several video games based on it already, which makes it useful to compare how mainstream stories like this are typically made into games with the method we advocate here. Second, while it may seem like a story world with Manichean values and lacking psychologically complex characters, it turns out to have more nuance and depth than any of the video games based on it may suggest, especially if we take into account the world of Ian Fleming's stories, which tend to be more character driven than their spectacle-driven filmic counterparts.

In order to determine the dramatic interactive possibilities of a story world, we start by listing as many verbs as we can think of that we can associate with it. The way we prompt this in our workshops is: "Tell me what is happening in these stories, but you are only allowed to say verbs". James Bond also allows us to focalize the verbs on a specific character. This is a typical verb set for this particular world (Table 4.1).

This verb set is by no means exhaustive, but it is representative enough for our purposes. This list already features a wide range of verbs; while most are focused on what the hero does (*spy, quip*), some are focused on what the hero is subject to (*torture*). Some are low-level verbs, meaning they are concrete actions, which might be directly tied to a button in a video game (*jump*). Some are high-level verbs, meaning they are complex, multipart activities that depend on context (*outsmart*). Other verbs involve physical actions (*shoot, drive*), others involve social actions (*seduce, gamble*), while others refer to the internal emotional state of the protagonist (*repress*). These verbs are taken from the different incarnations of the world, both in the novels and films, which vary wildly in terms of depth and content. For example, the 1970s films starring Roger Moore mainly involve the physical and/or spectacle-oriented verbs from this list (*quip, seduce, investigate, drive, outsmart*) whereas the more serious recent Bond films starring Daniel Craig involve these plus some of the more literary, psychological verbs on the list (*repress, betray, lie, love*). Let us identify the verbs on this list we might typically see in a James Bond video game (Table 4.2).

We've highlighted the verbs that are typically involved in many licensed James Bond video games, which have historically skewed more toward action

TABLE 4.1 Typical list of verbs associated with the fictional world of the James Bond stories

run	quip	dress	drive	save	repress
jump	torture	investigate	pilot	kill	hide
shoot	sneak	deduce	improvise	outsmart	betray
seduce	spy	escape	disguise	gamble	lie

TABLE 4.2 The verbs highlighted are typical of James Bond video games

run	quip	dress	drive	deceive	repress
jump	torture	investigate	pilot	kill	hide
shoot	sneak	deduce	improvise	outsmart	betray
seduce	spy	escape	disguise	gamble	lie

platformers and first/third-person shooters, from *James Bond 007* (1983) to *007 Legends* (2012). Games that involve more verbs from this set, like the text-based *Shaken, Not Stirred* (1982), which featured *investigate* and *deduce*, are an exception to rule. Since the landmark success of *GoldenEye 007* (1997), which is less famous for being a Bond adaptation and more for successfully bringing the first-person shooter genre to consoles, Bond tie-in games have almost all been shooter games that stray little outside the traditional verb set of that genre. One minor exception is *Everything or Nothing* (2006), a third-person shooter which featured explicit verbs like *spy*, *sneak*, and *outsmart* and very much presented itself as being an interactive Bond movie and less of an action-adventure game with a James Bond skin.

Thus, James Bond games, in general, haven't really embodied the dramatic potential of the character or his world, which is odd when one compares them with the film versions, which, even in their more serious incarnations, are still bombastic, mainstream action stories. Given the (heterosexual male) power fantasy standards of mainstream video games, it is surprising that verbs like *seduce* are not part of the verb set; it is even more baffling that actions related to stealth and espionage – a well-trodden area of game design with many fine examples, such as the *Splinter Cell* (2002–2013) or *Metal Gear* series (1987–2018) – is so underrepresented for a world that revolves around a spy.

One can easily imagine that the discrepancy between the range and diversity of verb sets between the games and the movies has something to do with how market risk is regarded in the world of mainstream video games once the expectations for a particular intellectual property have been set. Although we do not have room to unpack this in detail here, we want to point out that this discrepancy has more to do with the business culture of video games than with any inherent limitations of the art form itself, as evidenced by the appearance of all these verbs in other games. It is ironic that a James Bond pastiche like *Metal Gear Solid 3* (2004) prominently features verbs like *disguise* and *deceive* while so few James Bond games do. It is also disingenuous to claim that the mechanics of social maneuvering and seduction would be difficult to implement, when we can already see them in mainstream franchises such as Mass Effect. Thus, this is not a matter of generating innovative gameplay; it is about exploring different ways to abstract the world and providing new opportunities for gameplay in it. Seen through this lens, one can easily imagine a Japanese dating sim-style James Bond game that is only about seduction, where instead of gadgets and car chases, the point of the game is to figure out what to wear, what to say and how, when to bet or to bluff, and whether your martini should be shaken or stirred. Given that other games feature these mechanics, we can use them as starting points to explore emotion-driven characterization, and not just for the achievement of dating or spying or sneaking or lying – there is no reason we cannot imagine a James Bond game that approaches the thematic and emotional dimensionality of the latest film version of *Casino Royale* (2006), which was much closer to its literary source.

The point here is not that James Bond is high art, but that it does possess some literary dimensions which arguably have fueled its popularity as an enduring story world. It is not just car chases and explosions, even if those can be quite memorable. Video games based on this world theoretically have access to these dimensions but choose to avoid them. In contrast, the longevity of James Bond as a fictional character derives from the capability of the fictional world to incorporate the changing geopolitical conflicts, from the Cold War to the political tensions between the Eastern and Western hemisphere.[12] This failure to explore the verb set of the story world more fully may hint at why James Bond video games have stagnated in recent years. Verbs and the way that they simply and vividly cut right to the core of a world's drama, its conflict, and its systemic footprint make them an even finer tool for world-building in an interactive context.

This example shows how approaching dramatic, interactive world-building through verbs has been a cornerstone of our method for teaching narrative game design. We have honed this method down to a simple yet effective series of steps for making a world into a living interactive space while taking advantage of their dramatic core, which are as follows:

1. **Choose a preexisting world.** We tend to use films and historical situations, but it could be anything – comics, a TV show, a poem, a song, a historical situation. Anything that invokes a fictional world will do. One can go wider and choose a whole story world (such as Harry Potter), although a single text from that world will be just as effective to generate a verb set that represents the world – if the world-building is any good, it will be sufficiently expressed in a specific text. We do advise against (a) anything that has already been made into a video game or (b) action/adventure and superhero stories in general. This is because such stories tend to have a lot of verb overlap with traditional power fantasy video games (*punch, kill*, etc.), and therefore, finding the dramatic, emotional core is much harder and less immediate. Although it is not impossible, we discourage it as a starting world for this exercise. It is best to choose something that isn't a video game already and is unlikely to be made into a video game, such as the movie *Titanic* (1997) or the life of Elizabeth, empress of Austria. This will lead to the most vivid results.

2. **List as many verbs possible from that property.** This step is closer to brainstorming – write down all the verbs that come to mind related to the world, and don't narrow anything down yet. Go as wide as possible, and

include everything, even the verbs that may not sound totally right. Don't worry about who carries them out either. They can be the verbs of the protagonist or secondary characters, organizations, things done intentionally, things done accidentally, and from the ultra-concrete to the totally abstract. This should be a long list, so it is important to spend some time on it.

3. **Choose four that for you embody the core dramatic promise of the story.** The next step is to cull the list of verbs. This can be tricky, since there are many, many ways to break down a list of verbs to the right set of four. This is another step where abstraction becomes key, since it involves selecting what aspects of the world are going to be part of the game. Here is where the game designers flex their artistic muscles to decide what the dramatic core of the story is. Although there is no right or wrong way to do this, any verb sets that focus on verbs that strictly overlap generic video game verbs are discouraged, since they do not make the best out of this method. For example, the comic series *Watchmen* (1986–1987) is famously a multilayered critique of superheroes and the ideological baggage of the genre. You can mine all sorts of interesting verbs from it, such as *manipulate, lie, deceive*, yet it also has actions like *punch, stab, kill*. The 2009 video game based on the *Watchmen* film adaptation incorporates only the latter verbs, as a traditional violent brawler that looks like *Watchmen*. Given that the comic books only show violence to criticize it, this game adaptation misses the dramatic and ideological point of the original world, even if it is technically based on verbs that appear in the film and comics. The problem is not that *punch* doesn't belong in an interactive version of *Watchmen*; it's that the comic books depict punching in order to illustrate larger statements about regret and the moral corruption of vigilantism, among other things, which are some of the core conflicts of the world. Having *punch* and *regret* as a pair of verbs in this case would move closer to the artistic and dramatic territory of the original source material. Each world can present the opportunity to create many different verb combinations that yield artistically sound results. The job of the designer is to find the four that speak to them most.

4. **Make a paper prototype where the core game loop involves these four verbs.** The game can be whatever you want: a board game, a card game, a physical game. We discourage thinking about digital games, because the goal is to understand quickly how your verbs relate and whether they yield the sort of dramatic experiential result you had hoped. Card games can be an effective form, for example – the chosen verbs can be easily imagined as actual cards, so there is less of a tendency to get lost in the minutiae of game design that can obfuscate the actions the design is seeking. Seasoned game designers can use their best judgment as to what type of design they want to follow, whereas newcomers may have to try a few different approaches before they find one they like. Making sure the verb set includes a mixture of low- and high-level verbs is very useful to find the core mechanics – the

low-level verbs become the direct, concrete actions of the player (*lie*), and then the context and rules surrounding them are set up in such a way that the high-level verbs emerge naturally during play (*betray* . . . because you *lied* at the right moment). This is a good way to avoid getting stuck with verbs that are direct and easy to design for without generating a higher level dramatic complexity; it also helps dealing with verbs that are so high level and abstract that it becomes difficult to figure out how to have the player(s) directly engage with them.

5. **Choose the next best iteration of your game.** Once there is a prototype, the next step is to try to play it, see what works, and then play it again until the gameplay gets as close as our intended dramatic experience. What happens in this step is that by making a paper prototype, the fictional world is lost – the initial results tend to be abstract, because this process has zeroed into a limited set of actions and locations. The process is looking for a core, an essence, and tends to lose the rest. With each iteration of the game, it is important to ask oneself whether this core is what we intend or whether there is anything else that we want to include in order to bring back the fictional world or whether the four verbs we chose are the right ones for the kind of game we're looking for. For instance, in one of our workshops, a team made a game based on the papal conclave, the event where a new pope is chosen. This world is fascinating as a game, since it is a space for political intrigue and decisions. However, the team abstracted the world to a board game, where the key was moving and positioning on a checkerboard, which represented the Vatican. The verbs were *move*, *collect*, *group*, and *reveal*, which are generic board game verbs, rather than using those same actions to represent *ally*, *convince*, *betray*, and *announce*. The game became a strategy game based on space positioning rather than negotiating and dealing with hidden information. Although it was a well-designed game, it lost what made the world compelling.

6. **Decide what to do next.** The next step is deciding what to do with the game. The paper prototype can be a preparation for a digital version, although it is also possible to continue working on it as a nondigital game. At times, the team may not have the license to make a game on the world they made a game about – that's why works in the public domain and historical settings can be advantageous in this exercise. Even when the resulting game has lost the world that inspired it, as was the case of the papal conclave game, this method is also useful as a way to come up with new board game mechanics, if the goal is not one of world-building. Finally, this process need not even have a game as its final outcome. This exercise can be used with a traditional story that is in the middle of being written, like a first draft of a novel or screenplay; we have done this workshop with music composers and lyricists working on their shows. The goal of this exercise is to loosen one's imagination to figure out what is possible in the fictional world being created. Breaking

down the world into verbs, rules, and playing with them facilitates imagining scenes, conflicts, and scenarios that logically fit the world but one would have never have thought of otherwise. This is doing what J. K. Rowling and China Miéville do, but with the aid of game design as a writing tool.

In all the years of teaching this method, we have seen many examples leading to results that differ wildly from what might be expected from a game adaptation: a game based on the film *Gladiator* (2000) that isn't just about killing and survival but performing with honor and ethics so that Rome comes to love and respect the gladiator more than its own emperor; a game based on *Watchmen* whose core mechanics focused on trying to figure out which hero is pretending to be the villain by seeing through their empty moral rhetoric. There was even a *Brokeback Mountain* (2005) game where players had to wait until the wife was looking the other direction so they could steal a kiss from their boyfriend – a stealth dating sim.

This is what happens when we use the directness of verbs as an abstraction to parse a story world for dramatic design opportunity. Nothing is stopping story-based games from being as layered, emotional, and dramatic as stories in other media except the imagination and ingenuity of designers.

Bringing It All Together

As a final checkup on the prototypes created through this method, the final part of the exercise is to analyze how the verbs of the world help the players tackle the conflicts that we have identified in the fictional world. The character that the player is going to control must be equipped to tackle the conflicts of the world for several storytelling reasons. Derived from Stanislavski, the actions of the characters define who they are and how they tackle the conflicts with the world, so it is part of the characterization. The player-character also provides a point of view within the fictional world; this point of view is what can make the world compelling and worth exploring. Going back to the "fish out of water" trope, one of the reasons it is so recurrent is because it represents an outsider pointing at the contradictions, prejudices, and wonders that may have become invisible to the natives of a world because it is the only thing they know. In a similar way, by matching the verbs to the conflicts, game designers can provide an interesting point of entry into the game world.

By evaluating whether the verbs tackle the conflicts, we can also see whether the actions of the characters help the player understand and engage with the conflicts of the world or if the fictional world is just a generic playground for stock game actions. For example, the issue with some of the James Bond games listed above is that the verbs they feature are often the same as those of an action game – aim, shoot, run, drive – but none of these verbs relate to the information conflicts of the world, which would be the main job of a spy who plays a key role in gathering information relevant to international diplomacy.

As already mentioned, abstraction is still key to game design; the game does not have to include all the conflicts of the fictional world nor is it always feasible to do so. Different games may also tackle different conflicts of the world with different verbs. For example, going back to the world of *Battlestar Galactica*, there have been different licensed games based on the latest version. The video game *Battlestar Galactica* (2007) recreates the key missions of the first two seasons of the show as an arcade game, where the key verbs are *fly*, *shoot*, *pick up*, and *land*; a multiplayer mode of the game allows players to control a game as a Cylon, which included verbs like *hide* (as in going in stealth mode). This game uses the world of *Battlestar Galactica* to re-skin a typical shoot-'em-up game, without looking into what makes the world interesting and compelling and relies on the world itself and the brand to attract players.

On the other hand, *Battlestar Galactica: The Board Game* (2008) is an excellent example of narrative design, which shows how the process of design was probably closer to our own methodology. The board game is rather complex, but within that complexity, it does an excellent job of bringing some of the most memorable moments of the show into the gameplay. In board games, rolling the dice or drawing a card are not the verbs of the game, but they represent the possibility of carrying out an action. The game starts with tackling the environmental conflict; the players are humans in the eponymous ship, running away from the Cylons. The goal of the game is to reach Kobol before one of the key resources is depleted (fuel, food, morale, or population), which means that environmental conflicts dominate the game. Each turn, there is a crisis breaking out that players need to tackle with their actions; different players have different verb sets – pilot characters can *fly* and *attack*, technicians can *repair* ships, while the politicians and military can *make tactical decisions*. Each crisis is more ruthless than the previous one and threatens the resources severely; almost every turn, players will have to decide what kind of resource they want to lose.

To make things worse, and to make the conflict between humans and Cylons even more pressing, Cylon ships are chasing the Battlestar, and appear in waves every few turns, so the *Galactica* needs to be ready to make a hyperspace jump constantly in order to shake them off. Jumping to hyperspace is both a verb to tackle the environmental conflict (advancing in the space) as well as running away from the enemy. Last but not least, the game uses hidden information to create an extra layer of tension in the game – one of the players (or two if there are more than five players) is secretly a Cylon and will try to sabotage the ship without the other players noticing; halfway through the game, another round may reveal a new player is a Cylon as well. This mechanic embodies the key information conflict of the world (who is a Cylon?) as well as a personal conflict – how to act without giving away that you are the enemy, or how to change one's loyalty halfway through the game when a player discovers they're on the other side. The key verbs here are *reveal* and *hide* (information) as well as *betray* – the humans may want to know who the traitor is, while the traitor may want to wait until the right time to reveal themselves – which also brings about even more catastrophic crises to threaten the destiny of humanity.

The *Battlestar Galactica* board game does an excellent job of recreating the extreme challenges that the conflicts of the world generate, from the limited resources in a hostile environment to not knowing who to trust, resulting in exhausting game sessions full of drama and constant tension.

What makes the narrative design of this game remarkable is that even though it is a complicated game, its rules and mechanics are aligned with the conflicts of the world, with each character having a verb set that recreates their actions in the original show, so if one is familiar with the show, it is much easier to remember the rules (presented in a 32-page manual, no less). The verbs of the game and the players tackle the defining conflicts of the world, turning the drama of the show into gameplay, whereas the flight simulator tackled one the tritest conflicts in games (environment, factions).

Conclusion

This is only a summarized version of the methodology of our world-building and adaptation workshops; we have tried our best to communicate the pillars of our design philosophy. This methodology is intended for initial stages of prototyping, but its core concepts should be revisited throughout the process of designing a game.

One of the challenges of making a game based on a fictional world is that at times it is easy to resort to system changes in the design – adding scores, tweaking statistics, restructuring a turn. But making changes to make the game better at a systematic level sometimes means losing what those parts of the system mean and disconnecting them from the world. That's why checking regularly on how each part of the gameplay and each component represents the world is important to make the world come to life, whereas checking that the verbs address the conflicts of the world is a way to ensure that the dramatic action is relevant to it, rather than just recreating trite and tried mechanics. What we have proposed here is a method for innovation – finding new worlds, new characters, and new actions to turn into gameplay beyond what is out there. There are many games to be made based on worlds that one would not expect to make a game about: games about seducing, betraying, regretting, crying, and remembering, among many other actions. What we propose here is not to discard rules and systems as part of game design, but rather to focus on how they are meaningful and help create worlds with potential for dramatic action, so games can resonate emotionally with players.

Notes

1. See for example Gonzalo Frasca, "Simulation versus Narrative: Introduction to Ludology", in Mark J. P. Wolf and Bernard Perron, editors, *The Video Game Theory Reader*,

Routledge, 2003; Janet Horowitz Murray, "From Game-Story to Cyberdrama", in *First Person: New Media as Story, Performance, and Game*, Cambridge, MA: The MIT Press, 2004, p. xiii.

2. See Greg Costikyan, "Games, Storytelling and Breaking the String", in Pat Harrigan and Noah Wardrip-Fruin, editors, *Second Person: Role-Playing and Story in Games and Playable Media*, Cambridge, MA: The MIT Press, 2007.

3. From a chat transcript for Barnes and Noble and Yahoo! with J. K. Rowling and fans in March 1999, "1999: Accio Quote!, The Largest Archive of J.K. Rowling Interviews on the Web", available at www.accio-quote.org/articles/1999/0399-barnesandnoble. html.

4. Joan Gordon and China Miéville, "Reveling in Genre: An Interview with China Miéville", *Science Fiction Studies* 30, No. 3, 2003, pp. 355–373, available at www.jstor. org/stable/4241199.

5. See Chaim Gingold, "Miniature Gardens & Magic Crayons: Games, Spaces, & Worlds", Georgia Institute of Technology, 2003; Jesper Juul, "A Certain Level of Abstraction", Situated Play: DiGRA 2007 Conference Proceedings, Tokyo, 2007, available at www. jesperjuul.net/text/acertainlevel/; Clara Fernández-Vara, "From 'Open Mailbox' to Context Mechanics: Shifting Levels of Abstraction in Adventure Games", Proceedings of the 6th International Conference on Foundations of Digital Games, FDG '11. New York: ACM, 2011, pp. 131–138, available at https://doi.org/10.1145/2159365.2159383.

6. "Ultra-Realistic Modern Warfare Game Features Awaiting Orders, Repairing Trucks", *The Onion*, available at www.youtube.com/watch?v=yuTkgi7scKo.

7. Roger Caillois, *Man, Play and Games*, Urbana and Chicago: University of Illinois Press, 1961, pp. 14–17.

8. Clara Fernández-Vara, Borja Manero Iglesias, and Baltasar Fernandez-Manjón, "Stanislavsky's System as a GameDesign Method: A Case Study", Proceedings of DiGRA 2013: Defragging Game Studies, Atlanta, Georgia, 2013.

9. Bruno Fraschini, *Metal Gear Solid. L'evoluzione Del Serpente*, Vol. 2, Ludologica, Videogames d'autore, Edizioni Unicopli, 2003.

10. "Series Bible – Battlestar Wiki", available at https://en.battlestarwikiclone.org/wiki/ Series_bible.

11. Chris Crawford, *Chris Crawford on Game Design*, Indianapolis, Indiana: New Riders, 2005, pp. 166–167.

12. Tony Bennett and Janet Woolacott, *(James) Bond and Beyond: The Political Career of a Popular Hero*, 1st Edition, Methuen, MA: Macmillan Education, 1987.

5

SURVEYING THE SOUL

Creating the World of *Walden, a Game*

Tracy Fullerton

> Why do precisely these objects which we behold make a world?
> Why has man just these species of animals for his neighbors; as if nothing but
> a mouse could have filled this crevice?
> — Henry David Thoreau, *Walden* (1854)

Walden Pond and its surrounding woods may be one of the most documented
natural environments in the world, largely because of the depth of data collected by author Henry David Thoreau and from those following in his footsteps.
Known as a writer, a hermit, and a sometime activist, Thoreau was also a surveyor,
a naturalist, an inventor, and an erstwhile poet. His attention to the details of
this place, where he was born and spent most of his life, took the form of the
scientific and the aesthetic, the mundane and the metaphysical. In the 175 years
since Thoreau made the pond a cultural icon for solitude and self-reliance, many
others have followed in his footsteps, including myself. Naturalists and scientists
have recorded data about the plants and animals, the water levels and blooming
dates. Artists have captured the changes in the seasons, including the sounds and
senses of the environment. Philosophers and poets have nurtured and reaped the
ideas that Thoreau sowed here so long ago. Jane Holtz Kay writes, "If *Walden* is
the *Koran* of conservation, Walden, zip code 01742, is its embodiment. No parallel tract or body of water or place has so captivated the human imagination or so
taught us how to relate to the natural world from which we spring. Nowhere else
is there a literary memorial and monument of such breathtaking consequence. In
a world devoid of symbols and a landscape almost uniformly for sale, Walden is an
international shrine".[1]

I am little different from all those others who came here to find their own inspiration in Thoreau's writing and living at the pond, even though my goals might at first seem distant, or even contradictory to the themes of his writing. Since 2007, I have spent more than a decade designing and developing a playable virtual world in which we can all try our hand at Thoreau's experiment in living, can explore his ideas from wherever we are, and develop our own conclusions about life and how best to live it. This world, which I call *Walden, a game*, is a six-hour-long first-person video game set in a detailed simulation of Walden Pond and its environs circa 1845. When people first learn of my game, often their first reaction is one of surprise and confusion – "How can you make a video game about living in nature?" they ask me. Isn't that ironic? I answer that if it is ironic, it is exactly as ironic as making a film about living in nature, or singing a song about it, or writing a book about it. Making a game about living close to nature is simply using the medium of our time to investigate the essential questions of life, which are as pertinent today as they were when Thoreau asked them in his own way, in his own medium of choice. How best can we live our lives and the time we are given? When we strip our lives down to the minimum, what can we discover about what is really necessary and what is superfluous? How are our modern technologies and other "improvements" impacting the pace and quality of our lives? How can we seek the sublime among all the competing claims on our time and energy? These questions are as vital to us today as they were when Thoreau wrote about them, and it seemed to me to be an entirely natural thing to use the very technologies of our time to talk about them and to prompt players to consider the role of nature and time and quality of life in their real and virtual lives.

To begin this discussion of world-building in *Walden, a game*, I should note the unusualness of the subject matter in this instance of that practice. For the majority of world-builders, the process is one of invention, and the goal is one of fiction. The creation of full and interesting worlds, with rich, working systems at their core is, most typically, done in the service of using such worlds to tell interesting stories that take place in such worlds. In the case of *Walden, a game*, however, the process of creation for the world was deeply rooted in historical research, and the ultimate goal was the translation of a nonfiction experience rather than the creation of a fictional one. But as soon as I have noted these differences, I must also point out the fictional aspects of this nonfiction text. As a personal memoir, the book *Walden* makes no particular claims to objectivity. In fact, Thoreau insists in the very first words of the text on recognition of the subjectivity of what will come: "In most books, the I, or first person, is omitted; in this it will be retained; that, in respect to egotism, is the main difference. We commonly do not remember that it is, after all, always the first person that is speaking".[2] And so, it is important to admit that the text of *Walden*, first-person memoir that it is, was "made" and not simply reported. Thoreau claims that he "wrote the following pages, or rather the bulk of them" at the pond. But he also drafted and redrafted those pages for seven years after leaving the woods before publishing them as a completed narrative of his time there. In that final version, he concatenates his two years at the pond into one and includes episodes from before and after his time there as part of the time line. In many ways, Thoreau is the first "world-builder" to have crafted Walden Pond as we know it from his words and thoughts. Following in his footsteps, my own practice builds on his foundations; seeking to create a virtual representation of his own textual representation of this small corner of the natural world.

When Thoreau went down to the pond in 1845 to conduct his now-famous experiment in living a simple, self-reliant life in nature, Walden was not the cultural icon that we know it as now. It was simply one of many similar ponds in New England. Deeper than most, its ice was a useful resource for the area, cut out and sent to market in Boston. A popular fishing spot, it held perch and pickerel that made Thoreau exalt poetically, "Ah, the pickerel of Walden! When I see them lying on the ice, or in the well which the fisherman cuts in the ice, making a little hole to admit the water, I am always surprised by their rare beauty".[3] The woods surrounding the pond had been alternately denuded and replanted by the townspeople in their ongoing need for firewood and lumber, and the very land on which Thoreau built his retreat from society was a woodlot owned by his friend and mentor Ralph Waldo Emerson. The town of Concord was itself an early site of industrialization, with scars from the extraction of iron ore and smelting factories tracking through the surrounding areas.[4] In short, Walden Pond and its surrounding woods together was a place primarily used as a source of natural resources and not the celebrated source of philosophical retreat and natural beauty that we think of it as today.

And so, in the summer of 1845, when Thoreau began his experiment in living on the shore of the pond, there was no noticeable fanfare about it, other than his own. He went down to live in his half-finished cabin on July 4, a date purposefully chosen to represent the independence he hoped to find from the constraints of society and reliance on creature comforts. He was, at this time, at a crossroads in his life. He had tried teaching, losing his good job in the village school for refusing to use corporal punishment on the students. He and his brother John had also tried opening their own experimental school, but had not been able to make it work.[5] He had always thought of himself as a poet, but other than a few lines in *The Dial*, published by his friends and colleagues Ralph Waldo Emerson and Margaret Fuller, he had not had much success there either. He made his living primarily by doing odd jobs, since he was handy at construction, and doing surveying work.[6] Not too long before he retreated to the woods, his older brother John had died suddenly of lockjaw, shocking the Thoreau family and especially affecting Henry, in whose arms John had passed. The stoic Thoreau, unable to share his grief openly, worried his family when he too developed symptoms of lockjaw, but these were only sympathetic echoes brought on by loss.[7]

All this is to say that when Thoreau writes, in his now famous statement, that he went to the woods to "live deliberately, to front only the essential facts of life, and see if I could not learn what it had to teach, and not, when I came to die, discover that I had not lived",[8] he is not speaking metaphorically, but literally. He had experienced the deep shock of young death and had taken away from it the urgent sense that time, for us all, was a limited resource. "Time", he wrote, "is but the stream I go a-fishing in. I drink at it; but while I drink I see the sandy bottom and detect how shallow it is. Its thin current slides away, but eternity remains".[9]

As a game designer, Thoreau's experiment in living had always seemed to me to be a fascinating kind of game he had set for himself in the woods. It was a unique set of constraints, with an elusive goal, set in an interesting place to play and to challenge Thoreau to think about how best to spend this key resource, time, which is sliding away from us all every day. I had visited the pond a number of times as a child on family vacations and had read the book at various points growing up. Early on, I was captivated by the idea of building a cabin and living in the woods, then later, sparked by his thoughts on activism and civil disobedience. But finally, as an adult, sitting by the pond on a quiet drizzly day in 2002 when I, too was at a crossroads, I began to realize how the text functioned as a reflective surface, with its multitude of ideas and themes flowing and coalescing in such a way as to mirror back to the reader the very thoughts that they might need to hear on that particular reading of the book. Thoreau muses in *Walden*: "What if all ponds were shallow? Would it not react on the minds of men? I am thankful that this pond was made deep and pure for a symbol. While men believe in the infinite some ponds will be thought to be bottomless".[10] Like the pond, his book was made deep for a symbol, and it made me begin to think of what it might mean to craft a virtual version of this deep well of ideas. I began to imagine how I might create an interactive landscape that could reflect both the philosophical ideas and the personal experiences of Thoreau's time at the pond.

I have already mentioned that I am a game designer. Specifically, my focus as a designer is on experimental gameplay, and I have written extensively on methods for innovating in game design. I am also a professor of games at the University of Southern California and lead a research lab there, the Game Innovation Lab, where I have designed and developed a number of well-known independent games of which *Walden, a game* is one. But before all of that, back on the day in 2002 when I sat by the pond and thought about how it might translate into a system of meaningful play, I was, as mentioned, at a crossroads. At that time, I had been working in the game industry as a creative director and entrepreneur for just over a decade. I had recently closed my game development company and was thinking a lot about the nature of work, of time, and of play. Thoreau's experiment sparked in me a desire to create a world where we might all have the opportunity to "go to the woods" and discover the essential facts of life – not literally but virtually, and in a way that might turn the technologies that have so complicated our lives to a different purpose. I thought of a kind of game that might slow us down for a few moments each day, which might allow us to reflect on ideas that might inspire us to revalue the time we have and how we use it, a game that might reorient us away from conquest and competition toward contemplation and reflection.

I did not begin working on this idea at once. When I first thought of it that day in 2002 by the shore of the pond, it seemed beyond what I was capable of at the time. But five years later, having moved on from that crossroads to leave industry for academia, having by then formed the Game Innovation Lab, where our goal was to engage in design research for games, developing innovative concepts that pushed the boundaries of what games might become, I brought the idea to my team to see if we might dip our toes into Thoreau's well of inspiration. That was 2007. We released the game in 2017, ten years later, having spent a decade developing a vast virtual world out of our research into Thoreau's writings, his life and times, his relationships and beliefs. This essay is an attempt to deconstruct what we constructed and why – where we began with our world-building, the choices we made and why, and how we eventually created what would become a ludic collage of both natural and philosophical simulation, a space for discovery and reflection on Thoreau's ideas, his experiment in living, and the events that led him to make his quintessential sojourn at Walden Pond.

At this writing, *Walden, a game* has been released on a number of commercial platforms, including PlayStation, Xbox, and Steam. It has also been shown as a work of art in venues including the Cooper Hewitt Smithsonian Design Museum, the San Francisco Museum of Modern Art, the Smithsonian American Art Museum, the Concord Museum, and a number of other festivals and galleries. Successful as both an independent commercial game and an artwork, we also make the game available to educators free of charge with supporting curriculum. It is a unique project in that it was designed to cross the boundaries between independent game, art piece, and educational experience. So how did we create this simulated Walden that holds its own across these various domains, each with their own audiences and expectations? How did we begin the process of building Thoreau's world as a game, as a virtual landscape and experience? We began, quite simply, at the source: with Thoreau's own words and with his descriptions, both literal and visual, of the pond, as he knew it or thought of it. At the first meeting of our team, I brought everyone on the team a copy of the book, and we all began reading it again, underlining passages that spoke to us, and meeting to share our thoughts on how best to translate Thoreau's words.

Of course, one of the givens in our process was that the game would take place at the pond. There was never any question that some simulation of the actual pond itself would sit at the center of our world. But which pond? Not today's pond with its swimmers and soap suds clouding the shoreline. We wanted the game to reflect Thoreau's experience of the pond. And so, the best place to start was with his own detailed survey of its shape and contours. As Thoreau writes in *Walden*, "It is a clear and deep green well, half a mile long and a mile and three quarters in circumference, and contains about sixty-one and a half acres; a perennial spring in the midst of pine and oak woods".[11] He describes his careful process of surveying the depth of the pond early in 1846, before the ice broke up, with a "cod-line and a stone weighing about a pound and a half" and determining that the depth of it was 107 feet, "remarkable" he notes, in an area so small. His final "reduced plan" of the pond details not only the shape of the shoreline and coves but also includes profiles of the depth contours along its greatest length and again crosswise from Thoreau's own cove to the opposite shore.[12] And so, we were able to take the basic topography of our virtual pond from Thoreau's own survey and use it to craft the first and most visible aspect of our world. Sitting at the center of our virtual landscape, all else proceeded from the pond.

The terrain of the woods was a more difficult problem, since we knew that the shape of the land, its contours, and trails had definitely changed over time. So, while we began with modern US geographical data as a starting point, we also studied period maps of the trails and landmarks to get a sense of the lay of the land when Thoreau experienced it. There is quite a bit of confusion, for example, over just where his famous beanfield was. He describes it as being a lot of 11 acres "near" his house, which a farmer claimed was "good for nothing but to raise cheeping squirrels on".[13] Thoreau, with his trademark stubbornness, cleared the "good for nothing" lot of stumps and brush and planted about two and a half acres of it "chiefly with beans" but also a small part with potatoes, corn, peas, and turnips. It is the beans that readers remember, however, given Thoreau's fascination with them as a metaphor for the work of nurturing ideas, dedicating an entire chapter of the book to his endeavor to "know beans".[14] "It was a singular experience", he writes, "that long acquaintance which I cultivated with beans, what with planting, and hoeing, and harvesting, and threshing, and picking over, and selling them, – the last was the hardest of all, – I might add eating, for I did taste. I was determined to know beans".[15] Other than saying that the lot was "near" his house, however, he does not give other landmarks for the location of the field. Scholars have spent no small amount of time attempting to precisely determine the exact location, but for our purposes, a map made from the memory of Edward Emerson, grandson of Ralph Waldo Emerson, provided a location we could rely on closely enough.[16]

The size of the beanfield required some thought. According to our scholarly advisor, Jeff Cramer, "Thoreau planted 2 1/2 acres of beans in rows 15 rods long and 3 feet apart, approximately 146 rows, which adds up to a total length just under seven miles".[17] We knew that we could not create a beanfield this complicated for the game, since it would take too much time for players to engage with. Our days and nights had been shortened to a 15-minute cycle, and so tasks like bean farming and building the shelter had to be abstracted and shortened as well. And so we decided on a bean farm of six rows by eight plants, more of a garden than truly a field, just large enough to require a full in-game day for the player to clear or weed and laborious enough to require some rest in the middle of that task so that it could not be ground out too easily by eager gamers used to the farming mechanics of games like *Farmville* (2009). Similarly, the building of the shelter was reduced to a single hammering mechanic, one which would be simple enough to complete if players did a bit of maintenance on their shelter each day and yet

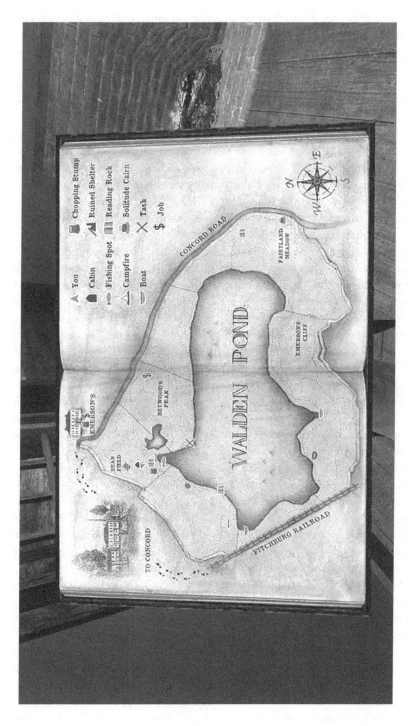

FIGURE 5.1 The in-game map of Walden Pond

difficult to grind out if players let the structure get into too deep of disrepair. The design of every task or interactable object in *Walden* required a deep dive into both textual and historical research but in the end relied on creative judgment as to how we could best abstract it into a meaningful inclusion in the world.

As another example of the way in which we based our choices on the text can be seen in the plants and the animals that are found in our virtual woods. As part of our initial process, one of the graduate students working on the project, Kyla Gorman, did a full indexing of the book, pulling out all the references to the natural world – plants, trees, animals, etc. She then did visual studies of the most-mentioned trees and animals in the book and of the kinds of edible plants that were available to Thoreau. Through this process, we were able to see what kinds of trees, plants, and animals would form the basis of our world. For example, there are 76 references to pine trees in the book, with 16 of them specific to pitch pines, seven to white pines, three mentions of yellow pines, and one mention of a red pine. Thoreau loved many kinds of trees for all their various beauties, but it was the "arrowy white pines" that he used to build his cabin, and he calls the pine wood behind his house his "best room" for receiving summer guests. In his journal, he calls the white pine "the emblem of my life".[18] And so, when building our world, we knew without question that two of the trees we would populate our virtual woods with would be pitch pines and white pines. We also included white and black birch trees, hickories, maples, oaks, hemlocks, spruce, and wild apple trees along with a variety of berries, such as blueberries, wild strawberries, smooth sumac, and Thoreau's favorite, huckleberries.

You might ask, why did we not begin with the flora and the fauna of today's Walden Pond? For one, they have changed, as environments do. You can still find the pitch pines and red maples, of course, but the pond of today is home to some different birds and flowers; different trails run through different stands of trees. Climate change has ravaged certain species and allowed others to take hold.[19] Human use of the pond has affected the composition of the water, the shape of the shoreline, and more. Walden Pond today is a very different place than it was when Thoreau spent his time there. Because of this, we made a choice at the outset that our goal was not to recreate today's Walden Pond and woods, but instead to simulate the pond and woods as Thoreau wrote about them. This design choice was important because our ultimate goal was that the player would experience *Walden, a game* as a translation of Thoreau's writing, of his worldview, of his experience at the pond.

For many world-builders, the palette they begin with is fresh, the world they are imagining can be anything conceivable. In J. R. R. Tolkien's classic discussion of the "subcreative" art of creating fantasy worlds, he emphasizes the importance of the labor and thought required to achieve "the inner consistency of reality". It is a kind of "Elvish craft" in his opinion, to create a "secondary world" commanding belief, one that he felt was best done in literature and not drama, since "very little about trees as trees can be got into a play".[20] But in our "play" we knew that

FIGURE 5.2 Early summer at the cabin (top, left); the pond at dusk (top, right); a fall day along the shore (bottom, left); and a surveying job (bottom, right)

we wanted very much about trees to be "got into" it. Ideas and musings about trees and nature fill Thoreau's journals and the book *Walden*. If we were to truly build his world, we must have trees and plants galore, and more, we must have a reason for the player to take notice of those trees and plants day by day, season by season as they walked our woods in the footsteps of Thoreau.

Early on in the conception of the project, I enlisted the help of Jeffrey Cramer, the curator of collections at the Thoreau Institute at Walden Pond, and we were able to ask Jeff specific questions we had about Thoreau's writings and life as we worked. One of the interesting things that we learned from Jeff was that Thoreau felt that four seasons were not granular enough to fully describe the rich set of changes the world of the pond went through over the course of a year. One of Thoreau's great pleasures was to visit particular trees and areas in all seasons, to see them transition from green to brown or yellow or red and back to green again. "I frequently tramped eight or ten miles through the deepest snow", he wrote, "to keep an appointment with a beech tree, or a yellow birch, or an old acquaintance among the pines".[21] And so, when we were laying out the world, we knew that we had to build it so that a player could create their own special relationships with our virtual trees over the course of the eight (not just four) seasons we planned to depict in our in-game year. Our game would, as much as possible, reflect Thoreau's fascination with the ever-changing wildlife around him.

In order to accomplish this, we created a single layout of our 3D terrain that dynamically changed its materials eight times over the course of our year. These materials include the deep greens and yellows of early summer transitioning through late summer into the reds and auburns of early fall; then to the bare browns and branches of late fall, and the crisp whites of early winter to the deepest snows of midwinter; and finally, from the muddy melt of late winter into the thaw and fresh greens of spring. As Thoreau writes of the seasons passing in his journal, "Live in each season as it passes; breathe the air, drink the drink, taste the fruit, and resign yourself to the influences of each".[22] We wanted our players to have this same sense of a world marching on through growth and change and transformation. And so, our world objects all maintain their underlying architecture, while their materials refresh as the seasons progress. By enforcing this underlying stability but also nodding to Thoreau's emphasis on the details of change, we were able to make our world a place that was both constantly refreshing with newly discoverable experiences but also make it a place that, as the player progressed, began to feel known, like a well-traveled trail. By the time players were ready to leave our virtual Walden, we wanted them, like Thoreau, to have a sense of the paths they had worn through the woods and through Thoreau's ideas: "The surface of the earth is soft and impressible by the feet of men; and so with the paths which the mind travels".[23] This ambition for the world to feel both new and then known was important to the overall arc of the game experience.

In addition to the seasonal changes, the world itself is designed as a kind of "objective correlative" of the player's relationship to our virtual nature. Underlying the basic experience are two core variables that the player must take care of: energy and inspiration. These two variables represent the delicate balance we must all strive to maintain between our physical and our spiritual (or aesthetic) health, as Thoreau calls them, the "mean" and the "sublime". In the game, they translate to the daily tasks of finding food, fuel, shelter, and clothing to maintain the "vital heat" balanced against the importance of seeking out the small wonders of nature and maintaining a state of "inspiration". Inspiration has a direct relationship to the look and feel of the virtual Walden. When the player is inspired, the world will feel fresh and vibrant – filled with color and sound and opportunities for interaction. When the player lets their inspiration fall, by ignoring their relationship to nature, the world around them will grow dull and colorless. The strains of music will fade to a minimal heartbeat, and the opportunities for interaction will diminish. The dullness of the world will remind us that we cannot simply grind our way through life, ignoring the natural world and the world of ideas and inspiration. These things are equally important as food and warmth to sustain us in our quest for a life well lived. This unique "reward" system was meant to prompt players to think about how their choices in the game affect the world itself, and their experience in it.

Unlike most games, *Walden, a game* is not about winning or losing, but instead about discovering and understanding. The things that can be discovered or experienced in it are both virtual and philosophical. The aggregate of these discoveries may lead the player to a real understanding of Thoreau's ideas and approach to living. The instances of trees and other natural objects that make up the virtual environment number in the tens of thousands, and as already discussed, the look and feel of these objects changes up to eight times during play. In addition to the looks of these objects, their bark and leaves, for example, each of them is also associated with a quote or a thought from Thoreau about that object. That quote or thought may also change as the seasons change. So, for example, if you come across a red maple in early summer, and you inspect it (a game mechanic for looking at it closely), you will find the following thought: "Sometimes you will see many small red maples in a swamp turned quite crimson when all other trees around are still perfectly green, and the former appear so much the brighter for it". Later in the year, if you inspect the same tree, you will find Thoreau's thoughts have turned to the morality of nature: "At the eleventh hour of the year, the tree which no scrutiny could have detected here when it was most industrious, flashes out conspicuous with all the virtue and beauty of a maple. We may now read its title, or rubric, clear. Its virtues, not its sins, are as scarlet".

This layering of Thoreau's thoughts into the very landscape of the world is one of the most important ways in which our design incorporates and unites his fascination with discovering in nature the answers to his questions about life. As players interact with the world, and the world changes around them, each of these quotes or thoughts is added to the player's in-game journal. Thoreau himself wrote in a journal constantly, producing 7,000 pages, or two million words, many of which would be re-crafted into his published writings.[24] So, as our players create their own journal of interactions with the world, they are, in essence, creating a procedural version of *Walden* based on their own gameplay experience. Ideas are found not only in the plants and animals but also in a series of glittering arrowheads scattered throughout the woods; a reference to the Native American artifacts that Thoreau was noted for finding as he walked the woods.

When, as part of my early research for the game, I saw some of these artifacts – arrowheads, ax–heads, and other tools that Thoreau found along his travels in Concord – I thought of this quote from Robert Richardson's biography of the writer: "Is it not singular that while the religious world is gradually picking to pieces its old testaments, here are some coming slowly after on the sea-shore picking up the durable relics of perhaps older books, and putting them together again?"[25] Thoreau was writing to Emerson and discussing the work he was doing to select portions of *The Laws of Manu* to be published in *The Dial*, but the quote sparked my interest in that it pointed to the way in which new readers of older texts might find deep value in them, picking them up, so to speak, and reconstructing their value in a new context. The earliest prototypes for the game all included the idea that players would search the game world for "relics" of the original text of *Walden*, and of Thoreau's other writings, and "put together" their own version of these as they played.

In the end, there are more than 500 unique textual "relics" to be discovered and collected by players in the world of *Walden, a game*. No single play though will reveal more than a fraction of them, however; and players are bound to develop their unique journal based on their own in-game experience. The pace of the game is also designed to give players a chance to review and reflect on the fragments they have discovered at the end of each game day. As mentioned earlier, we decided on a 15-minute day and night cycle for the game, with daylight filling about 12 minutes and nighttime about three. Brief transitions between day and night at the dawn and twilight hours give players time to adjust their plans accordingly as they work or wander the woods. At the end of each day/night cycle, a clock chimes in warning, and the players' journal opens. Now they have as much time as they like to peruse the day's entries. When they are finished, they can choose to "wake up" and continue to play. After three day/night cycles, the season advances, and as mentioned, the entire world and all the objects and text in it refresh to reflect the natural progression of time. This game journal, like the virtual world itself, is divided into the eight seasons of our year, and each begins with a thought from Thoreau to set the tone of that season. As we move into fall, for example, Thoreau muses aloud, in a paraphrase from his journal: "Summer is gone now, with all its infinite wealth, and still nature is genial to me. Though I no longer pluck so many berries on the hill, still I behold the same inaccessible beauty around me".[26] And later, as the late, hard winter sets in, we hear him tell us: "Is not January the hardest month to get through? When I have weathered that, I will get into the gulf stream of winter, nearer the shores of spring".[27] The arc of the year hangs on these seasonal quotes, telling as we hear, a story of "the change from storm and winter to serene and mild weather, from dark and sluggish hours to bright and elastic ones . . . a memorable crisis which all things proclaim. It is seemingly instantaneous, at last". Finally, as the year comes to a close, Thoreau rejoices that, "the sky appears broader now than it did. The day has opened its eyelids wider. The lengthening of the days is a kind of forerunner of the next season". We use these quotes as connective tissue between the procedural aspects of the journal, creating a time line based in the natural progression of the year and Thoreau's ecstatic witness to it.

From very early on in the design process, I knew that I wanted the arrowhead moments to be voiced. These moments make up a good portion of the text of *Walden* – approximately 25 percent of the book is included in the game. And so, the question of how to characterize Thoreau became of utmost importance in the design of the world and how it would feel to see it through Thoreau's eyes. Ultimately, the voice of Thoreau was played by Emile Hirsch, perhaps best known for playing the doomed Christopher McCandless in the film *Into the Wild* (2007). I felt extremely lucky to get Emile to play this part for such a low-budget indie game, since his performance fit perfectly into the version of Thoreau I wanted to portray – a young man, midtwenties, fresh with idealism but also tinged with the kind of youthful cynicism that often goes hand in hand with that idealism. When we think of Thoreau today, we often lump him in with a cannon of "old white men" of American letters. At the time that he lived and wrote at the pond, however, Thoreau was a young man, deeply skeptical of convention, even in his colleagues, such as Emerson. "Practically", he writes in *Walden*, "the old have no very important advice to give the young, their own experience has been so partial, and their lives have been such miserable failures".[28] Thoreau was destined to die relatively young, at age 44, and so I was adamant that we represent his voice as youthful, energetic, and full of the kind of vigor that would bring life to his words.

About 300 of the 500 quotes in the game are voiced, along with a series of letters that are sent to Thoreau by his various family, friends, and colleagues over the course of the game. In a world that is filled with so much solitude, I felt that it was important to have these human voices as part of the experience, engaging Thoreau (and the player) on subjects ranging from the personal and mundane to the political and poetic, since they provide both a narrative framework as well as insight into the society that Thoreau was stepping away from. As opposed to the natural elements of our world, this society is not to be found, for the most part, in Thoreau's book about Walden. Other than some oblique mentions of the shopkeepers and fellow countrymen of Concord, Thoreau speaks of no family or friends by name in the book. Vague allusions of visits from poets and wandering woodsmen let us know that he was not entirely alone by the pond, but not even his mentor and patron Ralph Waldo Emerson merits a mention by name in the text. And so, for this layer of content, we relied on biographical research and deep reading of what remains of the personal correspondence of Thoreau. Three hundred and thirty-eight of Thoreau's letters survive, and his letters to others, as well as letters about him to and from his family and friends, give insight into several important story lines that we have woven into the world of the game.[29] These include letters from Thoreau's sister Sophia, perhaps his closest sibling after the loss of John; inquiries from Professor Louis Agassiz at Harvard, looking for assistance with specimens from the pond; enthusiastic support for Thoreau's writing career from editor Horace Greeley in New York; calls for assistance to help fugitive slaves from abolitionist Bronson Alcott; and various notes and letters from colleagues such as Emerson, Fuller, and Nathaniel Hawthorne.

These letters, which are either edited from existing correspondence, or crafted in the vein of dramatic recreation, serve as a contrast or counterpoint to the players' time alone in the woods. Some are delivered to the cabin – like Bronson Alcott's requests to deliver supplies along the Underground Railroad – but most are to be found in town at the post office, the Thoreau home, or Emerson's home. The letters arrive season by season, unfolding their narrative aspects alongside the changes of the natural world. In the early days of summer, for example, we will find letters of good wishes for the start of Thoreau's experiment, recommendations for Thoreau from Emerson calling him "a fine brave youth of this town from whom I expect great things".[30] As the days and seasons pass, and the natural world reflects the more complex colors and feelings of fall and winter, so do the story lines revealed in these letters. Emerson's praise turns to critique: "Recall, if you will, that a frog was made to live in a swamp, but a man was not made to live in a swamp".[31] And sister Sophia's concern for Thoreau's health in the winter woods reveals an underlying grief that fuels that concern, dramatized in this in-game letter: "Even though you don't say his name aloud, I know you think of our poor brother John often, as do I".

Other story lines are tied to the myriad professions that Thoreau tried his hand at: odd jobs, surveying, and writing "for the magazines".[32] For example, players can choose to take on surveying jobs that are found at the post office. At first, these jobs seem a good solution to the necessity of making some money while also spending a great deal of time walking the woods and seeking inspiration. After all, the jobs take players to the far corners of the world, exploring the wild apple fields along the Concord road or following the length of the Fitchburg Railroad to the lesser-traveled areas of the woods. However, as the player continues on with these jobs, they may notice that their work is taking them to the most pristine and beautiful hidden areas of the woods ... now, instead of surveying an existing farm or lot, they are being asked to measure the lovely Fairyland Meadow for development, or even the coves of the pond itself. As Emerson mentions in a letter found on the cabin doorstep one morning, "Surveying does aid in the parceling up of your beloved woods. And yet, it is a living that could keep you while you write and live close to nature. A difficult choice, certainly". The dramatization of these concerns as part of our world was a conscious choice to involve players in some of the important themes of Thoreau's life. He was a surveyor, who loved the "the wild not less than the good",[33] and was conflicted about his own role in the carving up of nature for the use of society.

Similarly, Thoreau was an activist who preferred not to join any movement, at least until he could no longer stand by on the issue of slavery.[34] Along with the errands of mercy for fugitive slaves requested by Bronson Alcott, we have included perhaps the most famous of Thoreau's acts of resistance as part of the game world of Walden – his night in Concord jail. In the book *Walden*, Thoreau only briefly mentions this adventure. "One afternoon", he writes, "near the end of the first summer, when I went to the village to get a shoe from the cobbler's, I was seized and put into jail, because, as I have elsewhere related, I did not pay a tax to, or recognize the authority of, the state which buys and sells men, women, and children, like cattle at the door of its senate-house".[35] He is released the next day and straight away goes off huckleberrying as if the thing had little impact on him at all. We know, of course, that his deeper thoughts about the experience are to be found in the essay "Civil Disobedience", but if we were only to read *Walden*, we might think the arrest nothing but a nuisance to his berry-picking. For our world, we wanted the player to have some hints, as Thoreau must have had, that they might be disobeying the law, and even to have some choice as to whether they should try and pay those back taxes. We did this by posting a notice of back taxes due on the door of the player's cabin starting in late summer as well as a notice of public taxes in the post office. If the player goes to the general store to settle their taxes, they will find that they owe $9.00 – much more than they begin the game with, and a huge sum if they decide to try and earn it through odd jobs at two or three cents a task. The goal of this disparity is to bring to the forefront the player's decision as to whether or not to go to work immediately to pay taxes to the state and recognize its authority.

Even if they do start working to earn tax money, they are likely, by being in town, to be seized, like Thoreau, and put into the game's jailhouse all of a sudden, with no warning. Here they will find excerpts from "Civil Disobedience" to consider, along with posters recruiting volunteers for the Mexican–American War. Our jailhouse, like the one Thoreau describes, is simple, with "walls of solid stone, two or three feet thick, the door of wood and iron, a foot thick, and the iron grating which strained the light". Thoreau, while imprisoned, felt "struck with the foolishness of that institution which treated me as if I were mere flesh and blood and bones, to be locked up. I did not for a moment feel confined, and the walls seemed a great waste of stone and mortar".[36] We made a decision for our jail that seemed appropriate to the way the game treats the relationship between Thoreau's experience and the players. That is, you can choose to leave the jail when you like, by picking up an arrowhead on the window sill. However, you can also choose to stay in jail for as long as you like, protesting in-game the grievous moral failings of society. You will get very hungry and tired as you perform your strike, but you can watch the passing of the seasons from the window and remain partially inspired by this view and by the writings found in "Civil Disobedience". It is a way of allowing the player to make even more extreme choices than Thoreau himself, following in the footsteps of activists like Mahatma Gandhi and Martin Luther King Jr., as they themselves were inspired by Thoreau and his writings.

Ultimately, the world design of *Walden, a game* allows players to "live deliberately" in this virtual space and make their own choices about how best to do so. The task of creating this world, while differing in some key ways from the way in which builders of fantasy and fictional worlds approach their craft, also shares some important connections. Most importantly, the depth of inquiry into the aspects of its nature: its flora and fauna; its geography and terrain; its people and history; its cultural moment; and in this case, its relationship to the philosopher who first "imagined" and documented it. The world of *Walden, a game* was based on research, reflection, and synthesis of both the real and imagined, the current and the past, the personal and the social, and the fabricated and the natural. It is, among other things, a whole world built to illuminate for us the experience of this unique writer and his singular experiment in living.

Notes

1. Jane Holtz Kay, "Wall to Wall at Walden", *Nation* 246, No. 24, June 18, 1988, p. 867.
2. Henry D. Thoreau, *Walden: A Fully Annotated Edition*, Kindle Edition, editors, Jeffrey S. Cramer, New Haven: Yale University Press, 2004, Kindle Locations 157–158.
3. Ibid., Kindle Locations 3385–3387.
4. Austin Meredith, "A History of the Uses of Walden Pond", *Walden Pond History, American Transcendentalism Web*, available at http://transcendentalism-legacy.tamu.edu/authors/thoreau/walden/pondhistory.html.
5. Michael Sims, *The Adventures of Henry Thoreau: A Young Man's Unlikely Path to Walden Pond*, 1st U.S. Edition, New York: Bloomsbury, 2014, pp. 98–107.
6. Ibid., p. 155.
7. Ibid., p. 164.
8. Thoreau, *Walden: A Fully Annotated Edition*, Kindle Locations 1192–1193.
9. Ibid., Kindle Locations 1284–1285.
10. Ibid., Kindle Locations 3406–3407.
11. Ibid., Kindle Locations 2161–2162.
12. Ibid., Kindle Location 3424.
13. Ibid., Kindle Location 3403.
14. Jeffrey Cramer points out, in his annotated version of Walden, this phrase is a reversal of the common New England expression implying ignorance: "He doesn't know beans".
15. Thoreau, *Walden: A Fully Annotated Edition*, Kindle Locations 1986–1988.
16. Bradley P. Dean, "Rediscovery at Walden: The History of Thoreau's Bean-Field", *The Concord Saunterer, N.S* 12/13 (2004/2005), p. 86.
17. Thoreau, *Walden: A Fully Annotated Edition*, Kindle Location 5816.
18. Henry D. Thoreau, "Journal III: September 16, 1851 – April 30, 1852", *The Walden Woods Project*, September 15, 2016, available at www.walden.org/work/journal-iii-september-16-1851-april-30-1852.
19. Richard Primack, *Walden Warming*, Chicago, IL: University of Chicago Press, 2014.
20. J. R. R. Tolkien, and Christopher Tolkien, editors, *The Monsters and the Critics and Other Essays*, New York: HarperCollins, 2007.
21. Thoreau, *Walden: A Fully Annotated Edition*, Kindle Locations 3174–3175.
22. Ibid., Kindle Locations 6652–6653.

23. Ibid., Kindle Locations 3824–3825.

24. Henry David Thoreau, and Damion Searls, editors, *The Journal, 1837–1861*, New York: New York Review Books, 2009. Preface by John R. Stilgoe.

25. Robert D. Richardson, *Henry Thoreau: A Life of the Mind,* Berkeley, CA: University of California Press, 1986.

26. Edwin Way Teale, editor, *The Thoughts of Thoreau*, New York: Dodd, Mead and Company, 1962. All Quotes Are from Thoreau's Journal, with Date of Entry Noted, November 22, 1860.

27. Ibid., February 2, 1854.

28. Thoreau, *Walden: A Fully Annotated Edition*, Kindle Locations 225–226.

29. "About Thoreau's Writings", *The Writings of Henry D. Thoreau*, available at http://thoreau.library.ucsb.edu/writings_main.html.

30. Jeffrey S. Cramer, *Solid Seasons: The Friendship of Henry David Thoreau and Ralph Waldo Emerson*, Kindle Edition, Counterpoint, 2019, Kindle Location 249.

31. Ibid., Kindle Location 280.

32. Henry D. Thoreau, *The Correspondence of Henry D. Thoreau: Volume 1: 1834–1848* (Writings of Henry D. Thoreau), Kindle Edition, Princeton, NJ: Princeton University Press, 2013, p. 366.

33. Thoreau, *Walden: A Fully Annotated Edition*, Kindle Locations 2549–2550.

34. Sandra Harbert Petrulionis, *To Set This World Right: The Antislavery Movement in Thoreau's Concord*, Ithaca, NY: Cornell University Press, 2006, p. 91.

35. Thoreau, *Walden: A Fully Annotated Edition*, Kindle Locations 225–226, 2112–2114.

36. Henry David Thoreau, "Civil Disobedience", *Public Domain Books*, p. 17, Kindle Edition.

The essay originally appeared in *Sub-creating Arda: World-building in J. R. R. Tolkien's Work, Its Precursors, and Its Legacies*, editors Dimitra Fimi and Thomas Honegger, Walking Tree Publishers, 2019, pp. 1–15.

6

THE PLACE OF CULTURE, SOCIETY, AND POLITICS IN VIDEO GAME WORLD-BUILDING

Mark R. Johnson

World-building for me has always seemed to be a question of sociological real-ism: could this world, with these people (or other creatures), and these economic or political relationships, *actually* exist? Of course this might be a world which involves magic, the supernatural, the paranormal, the horrific, the science-fictional, the science-fantastical, or anything else: but within the rules of physical possibil-ity the world has set, could this world actually exist and function as depicted, or would it collapse under its own weight? As *A Song of Ice and Fire* (1996–present) author George R. R. Martin once famously asked (Gilmore, 2014), it's one thing to note that Tolkien's heir to the throne, Aragorn, might indeed have been a "good" or "wise" king – but what was his tax policy? The real world does not function on the basis of "goodness" or "wisdom", but rather on the complex interactions between many micro, meso, and macro factors of society, culture, economy, politics, people, places, geography, history, and much else: and there is no compelling reason to think that other possible worlds should be any different. Nothing breaks my own immersion in a fictional world more than realizing the world could not actually function if put into practice. It becomes as if the world in question is just a show put on for the sake of the reader, watcher, or player, rather than a living, breathing place which would continue to function *even if* we weren't reading, watching, or playing within it. But what does it mean for a world to be convincing in this regard, especially if this a world one *plays* instead of consuming more passively, with all the entanglements of agency and player unpredictability that go with it?

World-building on a significant scale is increasingly common in many digital games (Roine, 2016). In some cases, this means the creation of a universe at a resolution that might have given Tolkien pause, while in other cases, this means something far more compact. However, world-building with large-scale ambition tends to focus on a certain set of elements, and although these can appear to stand in for politics or culture, upon closer investigation, they fall far short of the kind of detail one might hope for in a complete world. Perhaps most central to this kind of world-building are maps: a planet (or equivalent) full of names for nations, cities, towns, natural sights, and so forth. These give the impression of a world which might be rich and varied, but where did all these places come from, and what are their connections in the wider story of this world? To answer these questions, such geographical details are often coupled with detailed histories relating the civilizations in question, along with religious beliefs or mythological ideas. These might tell us about great battles and noble (or otherwise) monarchs or the legendary founders of this city, this cult, that practice, that school. To further aid believability, some world-builders go further and create languages for their fictional worlds, although this can take on a number of forms. At one end of the spectrum world-builders try to make the names of locations within a certain culture generally similar or create a "language" through a simple substitution cipher, such as the Al Bhed language in *Final Fantasy X* (2001). At the other end of the spectrum, entire languages (or enough of a language to appear to be a complete language) might be constructed. These "conlangs" are good at creating a sense of otherness to the conversations of appropriate characters but are generally rarely integrated with other elements of world-building. This is not to suggest a requirement to follow a model of linguistic relativity – where one's language shapes one's understanding of reality (Lucy, 1992; Wolff & Holmes, 2011) – in world-building, but rather to note that there is none of the reciprocal determination of language, culture, and society in these worlds of the sort we tend to see in the real world. In a sense, these emphases speak to a certain historiography for these digital worlds: a historiography of great and grand events or people (cf. Furumoto, 2003), a historiography that is neat and clear, and brooks little ambiguity; the authors tell us what the world is, and they do so using the traditional tools of history retelling.

By contrast, what I understand as political, social, and economic world-building – more broadly, "sociological world-building" – is very rare in created worlds, digital or otherwise. This might seem like a strange observation given the above, yet I would propose it remains the case. I believe there are two issues here. The first stems from the cleanliness and clarity of the sorts of world-building listed above, speaking to a very modern, rationalistic, categorizing mindset. Rather like the great exhibitions of the Victorian era, designed to let attendees witness the entire world "concentrated in a mere point in space" (Young, 2009, p. 72), these explicit recountings of the history of an imagined world leave – somewhat ironically – very little to the imagination. In a sense, they are a kind of taxonomic project, designed to make clear everything the author has imagined about this world and impress the player or reader with the scope and scale of their imagination. However, even if this level of detail and information might begin to mirror that of the real world, its presentation does not: it implies a degree of certainty unknown even in the contemporary technological world, let alone the quasi-historical worlds much world-building fiction is set within. These sorts of constructions form a historiography without ambiguity, or if there *is* ambiguity, it is the sort of ambiguity which is captured and rationalized in lines like "Her final fate was unknown", or "He travelled to the South and was never seen again". A small part of the vagueness of real history is captured by these phrases, but in doing so, is made as certain and concrete as anything else.

The second issue is that alongside this clarity and crispness of much world-building, the level at which world-building often takes place is both at a macro scale and in a way that reflects the dominant forms of describing the world prior to the last few decades: as above, an emphasis on the most important people, the most important battles, the precise recounting of geography and history. Or, to put this another way, there is rarely much in the way of *social history*. A full look at the rise of social history as an intellectual movement, and its profound effects on how we think about the world, is far beyond the scope of this essay (see Fairburn, 1999; Fass, 2003; and Gunn, 2006). Nevertheless, the greatest benefit of social history is, and has always been, putting people – and their interactions, and the roles of social forces – back into the telling of history, or the description of a world. It is rare in world-building, in digital games or otherwise, for us to hear too much about clothing styles, family life, employment, dialects, class, architecture, migration, literature, music, visual art, or trade, yet these would be integral to the lived experiences of everyone within that world and would have surely shaped their existences far more than the grand political events, geographical distinctions, or historical moments that world-builders tend to focus on. Yet in order to create a world which is convincing in social, political, and economic terms, these dimensions are essential.

Both these points are not to say no digital games have attempted sociological world-building as I understand it; complex and contingent, rather than clear and unambiguous, and emphasizing social history (or at least allowing room for social history) compared to a history closest to the "great men" framing of the past. It is, however, rare. As such, in this essay I want to look at what a central dedication to political, social, and economic world-building might look like in a digital games context. I believe these are essential parts of any convincing fictional world (outside of worlds with a smaller or more limited "scope" of creation), have immense potential for creating a believable world the player is able to move through and interact with, and also bring with them opportunities for developing unusual or distinctive game mechanics of a sort we rarely see in other games. To properly examine these factors, I want to look first at a number of games which have developed these elements of world-building unusually well, often to an unusually high level of detail. Specifically, I will look at the worlds of one half of the *Command & Conquer* series by the now-defunct Westwood Studios, a number of the titles released by Stockholm-based grand strategy game developer Paradox Interactive, and the so-called *Soulsborne* series of games by Japanese developer From Software. I will then consider my own creative work in this area, *Ultima*

Ratio Regum (2011–present), and look to relate something of the design process for creating a game rich in sociological world-building *and* which is procedurally generated – which is to say, the game and its world-building are created anew, algorithmically, on each instance of play. In summary, my goal with this essay is to emphasize the importance of this kind of world-building, critically assess some strong case studies in this area, and outline some initial ideas about how to develop this kind of world-building – whether in digital games or elsewhere – as a means to creating fictional spaces with a deep sense of sociological verisimilitude.

Sociological World-building in Digital Games

First, I want to consider a series of real-time strategy games which excelled in this kind of world-building. The *Command & Conquer* (1995–2012) games, by now-defunct Las Vegas developers Westwood Studios (later owned by Electronic Arts), are known for two parallel story lines. New releases would generally alternate between the two as time went by. The first, generally known as the "Tiberium" games, focused on a near-future real world being terraformed by a valuable but deadly alien mineral – likely inspired by Frank Herbert's seminal *Dune* series – brought to Earth via a seemingly rogue meteor, the resulting asymmetric wars and power struggles between a global militarized UN-esque force and a decentralized quasi-religious/quasi-"terrorist" opposition, and later the mysteries surrounding the origin of Tiberium and humanity's potential larger place in the universe. This half of the series was generally played straight and focused heavily on exploring the effects of these wars and the effects of this alien mineral on global and national societies, economies, politics, and militaries. The second, known as the "Red Alert" series, was a tongue-in-cheek alternate history where Soviets and their allies, rather than Nazis and their allies, fought in opposition to the Allies in the Second World War. Whereas the former generally sought technological realism even within an increasingly science-fictional setting, the Red Alert series was comfortable deploying weather control devices, time travel, mind-controlled giant squid, towering Japanese mecha, weaponized dolphins, and laser battles on the moon (Johnson, 2015; Goodfellow & Cybulski, 2016). The outlandishness of many of this second set of *C&C* games was certainly much of their playful appeal but prevented much serious world-building. As such, it is the effective sociological world-building specifically of the Tiberium games I want to look at here.

In the Tiberium series, the player controls commanders on two sides of a conflict. On one side is the "Global Defence Initiative" or GDI, a supranational military body resembling a combination of the contemporary real-world US army and UN peacekeepers. On the other side is the Brotherhood of Nod, a shadowy cabal of decentralized global groups who represent something between a religious cult, a terrorist organization, a freedom fighter group, and an anti-capitalist paramilitary organization. The games commit extensive time to constructing these factions not just as opponents to play against but as elements of a fictional world which are complex, contested, and consistently engaging with elements of the game world only ever "off-camera". Indeed, traditional history about these two factions is relatively absent: almost nothing is written about GDI's formation or evolution, and even less about Nod; however, the games tell us much about who follows them and why, how their ideologies intersect with what we would now call the Global North and the Global South, the financial resources each draws on and the sources of that wealth, the countries and territories each holds sway over, how they interact with global media outlets, and much more besides. The games treat these factions not so much as powerful military actors, but rather more as social forces reshaping the world around them through their conflict and the resource which drives it.

The commitment to this sort of world-building detail is even reflected in minor details, such as the buildings the player can construct playing as each side (Figure 6.1). For example, Nod "produce" their vehicles from an airstrip, where they fly in lightly armored vehicles from shady global arms sources; by contrast, GDI construct their (more advanced and more heavily armored) vehicles directly, reflecting their far greater ability to deploy significant economic resources and cutting-edge technology. Detail of this sort is also geographical: the GDI campaign involves the player attempting to secure Europe – a traditional NATO stronghold in the real world, a major part of the Global North, and as the game even states, a central source of GDI funding – while the Nod campaign entails persuading the disenfranchised postcolonial nations of Africa to unite behind their banner. Through these campaigns we see the political effects of this ongoing war on various countries, their leaders, their politics, and their media outlets; we even get some sense of how the GDI is funded, and the positive public feeling that continued funding is contingent on, alongside some idea of how Nod deals with both internal dissent and external relations. All these elements are certainly not essential for gameplay, nor are they presented as fixed elements of the world, which are being changed; we only learn about them through the process of playing the game and having an effect, which allows us to deduce a greater sense of how this world functions.

However, gameplay also builds the world and the player's experience. For example, in the final Nod mission, the player seizes control of GDI's "superweapon", a space-based laser platform, and has the ability to use it to destroy one of four possible world icons: the White House, the British Houses of Parliament, Brandenburg Gate, or the Eiffel Tower. The point is explicitly to deal an ideological blow against GDI, and the final credits sequence shows us a news report reflecting on the impact on GDI's loyal countries from this apparent accident, or even possible betrayal. The game once again shows its commitment to looking at the sociological complexities of how the conflict evolves over time. In the later games in the series, after Tiberium has destroyed much of Earth, the worldbuilding shifts to focus on the planet's ecology, the social effects of the widespread movement of population, growing gulfs between the rich (who can afford safety) and the poor (who cannot), and so forth. These elements of the world emphasize

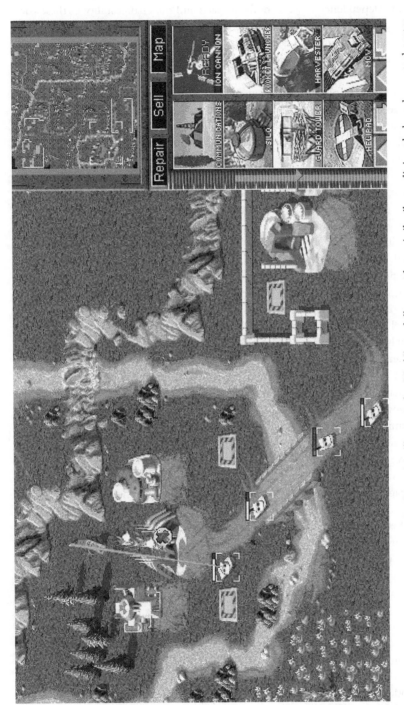

FIGURE 6.1 *Command & Conquer.* GDI forces in yellow attack a Nod "temple" – a nuclear missile silo, a religious hub, and a control center in one – while moving around surface-to-air missile sites designed to limit GDI's air supremacy

the interdependence of all its different parts and the changeability of these parts: nothing is set in stone, and the future of the world remains contested between both human factions and nonhuman forces. As such, throughout the games, this world-building is closely mirrored in the gameplay we perform: the politics and the socioeconomic order of the world are not just a backdrop, but actively integrated into the player's actions and potentialities. Everything we see seems to emerge organically from the unpredictable interactions between the factions, not from any intended teleology or direction: the world is a deeply sociologically convincing one, precisely because it focuses so much on chains of cause and effect and eschews any larger or grander narratives in the process.

Second, I want to consider many of the titles by Swedish developer Paradox Interactive. Of all their series, Paradox is arguably best known for its *Europa Universalis* (2000–present) games, in which the player controls a nation from the 15th century until the 19th century, without any explicit goals. Traditionally, the player is implicitly expected and encouraged to expand and grow their influence, although as with other Paradox games, the player is free to create their own objectives. The game presents an extremely complex interweaving of political systems and military forces, which can play out in almost any number of ways. Similarly, their *Crusader Kings* (2004–present) series, set in a slightly earlier time period, places the player in control of a single individual from a noble family (and upon their death, the player controls their heir, and so on), but rather than a purely "great men" model of history, the game is skilled at demonstrating how the fates and decisions of individuals – within a political-economic system where the individual was paramount – did not just shape the outcomes of wars and the creation of nation-states, but were also reciprocally shaped by those same events. For example, religious conflict might determine who *can* marry, and therefore who *does* marry, and therefore what nations form alliances, and therefore which go to war, and so forth. One of the most distinctive points of the *Crusader Kings* franchise is thus its detailed depiction of how politics – in Europe and Asia in the period depicted – were heavily contingent on marriage alliances, and thus the associated interweaving being individual and family lives and the wider political, economic, and social fates of nations (Figure 6.2).

The *Hearts of Iron* (2002–present) series, meanwhile, offers equally detailed simulations of the Second World War, in which players can take control of any of the primary antagonists and play to produce very different resolutions and even entire alternate histories. As with the other games, this is based on real-world data – the names of generals, the distributions and strengths of soldiers, the technological abilities of the belligerents, and so forth – which can then play out in an almost infinite number of different ways. In the same style as *Crusader Kings*, these games present us with deeply complex networks of sociological elements, allow us to play with them, and ensure our playing is consistent and logical. Paradox's *Victoria* (2003–2010) series is set during the Victorian period, and unlike its other games where war is a central component of gameplay, these emphasize even more than their Paradox cousins the functioning of a country's economy and the process of industrialization. Most recently, Paradox has released *Stellaris* (2016), a grand strategy science-fiction game. Players take control of a heavily customizable newly interstellar civilization and can expand and grow their civilization in almost any way they could imagine. There are no clear objectives in the game, except perhaps survival (although in some cases even failing that can be considered a narratively acceptable ending), and so players can easily create their own objectives: to create an empire which enslaves all other species, a civilization where all its inhabitants spend most of their time on powerful relaxing drugs, an alliance of different cultures which stretches across the galaxy, a vast crime syndicate which monopolizes certain resources, or even a machine civilization dedicated to protecting and preserving organic life. In all these games, therefore, the player is given a small amount of control over a few elements (a person, a country, or a faction) of a hugely complex sociological simulation. Indeed, Paradox's games have become notorious for being extremely challenging to learn as a result of so many intersecting elements (Kaiser, 2013; Walker, 2016), with many players simply giving up altogether.

In contrast to the *Command & Conquer* series we just considered or the *Soulsborne* games we will look at shortly, most of Paradox's games have an inherent "advantage" through the use of real-world individuals, countries, cities, events, and so forth. They are creating an adaptation of the real world and building it into a functional "doubled" world with a complex set of rules, designed to mirror – in almost all cases to the greatest extent possible – the real social, political, or economic functions they emulate. In historical games, for example, little effort is made to "balance" different civilizations: some are simply more technologically advanced, more militarily powerful, while others have unique traits or characteristics that either help or hinder a player's efforts to utilize them. The detail and sociological meticulousness of their "world-building", therefore, emerges out of the *possibility* for these systems and their known starting conditions to evolve in strongly divergent directions. This is only possible because the worlds are so intricate and with so many mechanics and interactions being present. These are not presented as unchanging states of being as is in most world-building, but rather the sum totals of a hundred thousand different elements, every one of which will start to "decohere" and change as play proceeds. This ability makes these games exemplary examples of sociological world-building: millions of contingencies, a coherent and consistent system which generates unpredictable outcomes, and a huge number of variables implicated in the economics and societies within the game; and consequently players experience a tremendously detailed world which – within the confines of computer logic – behaves as one might expect a world to behave according to the rules for that world we've been shown.

Third, alongside *Command & Conquer*'s Tiberium real-time strategy game series and many of Paradox Interactive's most successful grand strategy games, I also want to look here at the so-called *Soulsborne* series, developed by Japanese studio From Software. Although very different in thematic settings, these games all

FIGURE 6.2 *Paradox Interactive:* The player decides how to deal with a distinct historical and cultural event, contingent on the civilization the player controls and many other factors

offer action-based role-playing, extremely detailed worlds, famously challenging combat, and cryptic narratives. Beginning with the cult hit *Demon's Souls* (2009), the series then moved into a trilogy of *Dark Souls* games (2011, 2014, 2016) in a shared universe; a separate release titled *Bloodborne* (2015) set in a different world; and more recently, another new fictional world for players to explore in *Sekiro: Shadows Die Twice* (2019). All were critically acclaimed, with *Dark Souls* and *Bloodborne* in particular being now commonly cited on lists of the "greatest games of all time". In turn, all but *Dark Souls 2* – shorn of the director of all the other games, Hidetaka Miyazaki, due to his focus at the time on *Bloodborne* – have been widely praised by a large and enduring base of dedicated players, as committed to unraveling their cryptic worlds as they are to defeating the games' challenging enemies and labyrinthine-level designs. Miyazaki has famously described that this storytelling and world-building method originated when he was a young consumer of English-language fantasy novels: knowing some English, but not fluent in the language, he was forced to make up the missing details he could not gather by reading a text (Parkin, 2015). This is reflected in the storytelling, and more importantly here, the world-building: the player is given *just* enough clues to piece things together, but this often takes time; fully uncovering the plot of *Bloodborne*, for example, took many months, despite millions of players around the world. The player gets the strong impression that everything they might be able to know *is* there, but as in the real world, they are only getting a partial impression of the world's history based on whatever artifacts or ideas have survived down through the ages. It is this feeling which makes these games important for our consideration of sociological world-building.

Inspired by Miyazaki's childhood literary experiences, performing world-building through these brief slivers of information is highly distinctive. For example, in *Dark Souls* we encounter a great city with two staircases that lead up to its most important building; one built for the giants we know by that point in the game once inhabited it, and one for the humans who lived alongside them. Nothing is ever said of this staircase, and it is easily ignored, but it immediately both says a lot about the game world and intersects and sheds new light on everything else the player might have learned up to that point about the humans, or the giants, of that fictional world (Figure 6.3). *Bloodborne* is equally replete with these minuscule details which construct a complete world: almost anything, ranging from the clothing worn on long-dead nonplayer characters (NPCs) to the precise visual appearances of individual items the player collects, are all designed to give just the slightest of clues, and encourage the player to connect those to others previously acquired. These are all seemingly trivial pieces of world-building, but the *Soulsborne* worlds are built out of hundreds or even thousands of these pieces, all of which are designed to show the existence of a world specifically designed to be lived in by the creatures we've seen living in it. In a broader sense, this is an approach applied to the *Soulsborne* games' gameplay as well: their worlds rarely resemble "levels in a video game", but are much more like slices of an alternate reality, quite specifically *not* made for the player to easily navigate, which the player's character just happens to find themselves in. Again, it is as if each world has not been put there for the player, but must be navigated nonetheless: these elements are thus all part of "preserving a sense of mystery and gesturing towards a whole that escapes the player's conceptualizing grasp" (Vella, 2015).

This also has another effect, which is the temporal reversal of how the world appears to have been built. To put this another way, it genuinely appears that long, complex, and contested sequences of events have led up to the present state of affairs, rather than a present state of affairs having been decided by the world-builder(s) and then historical events inserted to lead up to a predetermined end-point. Even if this is not *actually* the case and the world-building process in the *Soulsborne* games did begin with its intended end state (which we must assume to be the case), the illusion is unusually convincing. It is made real by the meticulous attention to the smallest minutiae of the settings' details, the focus on how ideological or artistic or religious or social ideas spread through a society and an acknowledgment often central to the games' inscrutable narratives that history rarely tells a "real" story of how we got to where we are now. These are worlds where the flow of "history" and its impact on the present are just as messy and contested as they are in reality, yet just as visible for someone who invests the time in seeking out their signs and clues. There are buildings in strange places, ante-chambers built at a later date, layers upon layers of structures and aesthetic styles, historical records which disagree, places which seem genuinely forgotten until the player stumbles upon them for the "first time". These are worlds which are *messy*, unclear, and uncertain and which display the same strata of change and forgetting that we see within the real world. These concepts are distinct from the concepts I sought to highlight in the previous two series but show another successful path to convincing sociological world-building.

As such, I propose these three sets of games have several things in common. First, they satisfy the requirement of uncertainty: that we should not be presented with a single coherent historical narrative defined by its inflexibility, rigidity, and certainty of record-keeping; instead, we should be faced with worlds where the facts are contested, opaque, or both. In all these, many important matters are vague and uncertain to both the player and the world's characters, things take place off-screen suggesting the existing of a wider world and therefore a world which isn't just there for the player: in other words, it feels real (relatively speaking). Second, these are worlds committed to producing a *social* history, not just an itinerary of rulers and the cities they conquered (or whatever), but rather a deep commitment to social history, *and* a world where these are not incidental features, but are essential to telling a rich and detailed story. In the Tiberium series, much is left unexplained to both the player and the characters within the game world, yet the games tell complex narratives through their world-building and give a strong sense of the contested political, geographical, economic, and social landscape of their worlds; in the *Soulsborne* games the in-game characters are generally almost

FIGURE 6.3   *Soulsborne*: Two staircase sizes in *Dark Souls 3* (and *1*), a typically subtle yet
integral piece of world-building employed by these games

completely ignorant of their "true" history or the nature these of their world,
and the player must piece it together not from great texts about ancient wars but
the subtleties of architecture, clothing, morphology, and the like, while in many
of Paradox's games, tens of thousands of moving parts construct a world from
the bottom up, rather than from the top down. These worlds feel as if they have
existed before the player arrived and will continue to exist after the player is gone,
because so many elements beyond the player's actions – however heroic or dramatic they might be – are what construct the world.

Ultima Ratio Regum and Generating Social Histories

I've now looked at three game series which exemplify what I mean by political,
economic, and social world-building within digital games. In different ways, *Command & Conquer*'s Tiberium series, many of Paradox Interactive's games, and the
Soulsborne franchise exemplify the sort of sociological world-building – political,
social, and economic – that interests me. For the rest of this essay, I want to take a
critical look at my own contribution to this sort of world-building and reflect in
doing so on the sorts of design choices, and the sorts of gameplay mechanics, one
might elect to develop in order to create a world of this sort.

For the past eight years I've worked on a game called *Ultima Ratio Regum*, a
Latin phrase, which translates roughly as "The Last Argument of Kings". This
was a phrase that Louis XIV famously had engraved on the cannon built during

his reign, the point being that when all traditional arguments fail, monarchs still have one "argument" left: that of irresistible force. In a game which has moved significantly from its original intentions, and one which has become far more interesting to a far wider range of people than I ever intended, this is no longer an especially appropriate name. Indeed, many question the name's applicability and struggle to remember it, two issues which do not seem especially conducive to the success of a creative product. Nevertheless, it is certainly too late to change it now. At time of writing I am about to release version 0.8, which has now been around four years in development, having taken several orders of magnitude longer to create – but also being appropriately larger in scope – than any of the preceding releases up to this point. This might be the final major release of the game, or it might not; much has changed in the eight years since I began this project, and other creative projects beckon. If it is the final release, *Ultima Ratio Regum* will not have reached its initial gameplay goals but will certainly stand as one of the most detailed world-generation systems ever developed.

Set in an alternate Earth around the time of the Scientific Revolution and the Renaissance, *URR* offers the player an extremely detailed world to explore, which is historically accurate while also extrapolating about other potential paths human society might have taken. One of the defining features of *URR* is that every time a player starts a new game, an entirely new world – but always in keeping with these parameters – is generated by the game, meaning that nobody, including its creator, can ever know what sort of world will be generated. To do this the game uses a set of techniques which broadly fall under the label "procedural content generation" (Grinblat & Bucklew, 2017; Karth, 2018; Salge *et al*, 2018). This refers to the writing of algorithms and systems which – within boundaries set by the designer – are unpredictable and can create in-game content which cannot be predicted until its creation (Johnson, 2018). Within each unique world, players explore, learn about the world, enter buildings with distinctive architectural styles, talk to potentially millions of algorithmically generated characters, uncover and explore the planet's landscapes, and examine clues generated by cultural items, ranging from flags to chairs, weapons to religious altars, and clothing to doors (Figure 6.4). Players are able to closely examine anything they encounter within the game world, enter any building, talk to any character about several hundred different topics, and generally explore the full depth of the generated planet in both geographical and social terms. The more they learn about the complexities of the world, the more they can talk to characters about it, and the more characters might tell them about it.

Although this began as a pet project around the time I started my doctoral work – since taking on only a single multiyear project was apparently insufficient – it rapidly picked up traction with roguelike players and strategy game players. At the time of writing, well over 100,000 people have downloaded the game, and many have been kind enough to leave regular comments, feedback, information about bugs, and so forth. Despite the length of development time, from the very beginning one of the core goals of the project was to implement world-building with gameplay as closely as possible and to make sure more "abstract" elements of world-building (such as dialects or languages) could, in some way, manifest themselves physically in the game world and thus show their effect on the cultures of the generated planet. Characters within the game world should disagree with each other, or dislike each other, or tell the player different things, depending on their personal backgrounds, religions, cultures, and many other similar elements worked into the game's systems. The game has also garnered attention in the academic literature on both procedural content generation and world-building – although I would not define myself as a computer scientist, it has been a deeply satisfying experience to take both of these concepts in both technical and artistic directions rarely explored before.

There are six parts of this I want to briefly talk about here, which I have come to think of as contributing to the political (two aspects), social (three aspects), and economic (one aspect) world-building of the game's procedurally generated planets. These are the detailed generation of governmental forms and different sorts of buildings and infrastructures which support them (political); the spread of religions with complex ideological entanglements, beliefs, and influences on different governments and cultures (political); the generation of a wide range of character faces and appearances which vary widely across geography and culture (social); millions of different potential clothing styles for in-game characters including ones for the player to wear (social); procedurally generated dialects for individuals from each different in-game culture as well as the creation of unique naming conventions for different cultural groups, rather than the creation of "languages" of the sort discussed earlier (social); and finally the game's implementation of diverse currencies with different relative values, cultural associations, and aesthetics which appropriately mirror the cultures of the nations which use them (economic). These six elements are not exhaustive of the game's world-building – although some of these six are close to unique within the digital games space – but are indicative of the elements that went into constructing the kind of sociologically detailed world the game required.

Governments and Infrastructure (Political)

One of my core initial goals for *URR* was to build a functioning political world, not one akin to games like those in the *Democracy* (2005–2013) series where the politics are the gameplay, but rather a world whose politics create the world the player explores. In a broad sense, civilizations in *URR* can be ruled by a democratic or quasi-democratic parliamentary system with delegates being sourced from across the culture; an absolute monarchy with varying potential distributions of power between the constituent parts of that civilization; a theocracy led by a pope or equivalent who rules from a cathedral and has a powerful and sometimes absolute influence on the religious beliefs of that culture; a stratocracy where the military control the nation (with appropriate attendant effects on the society and

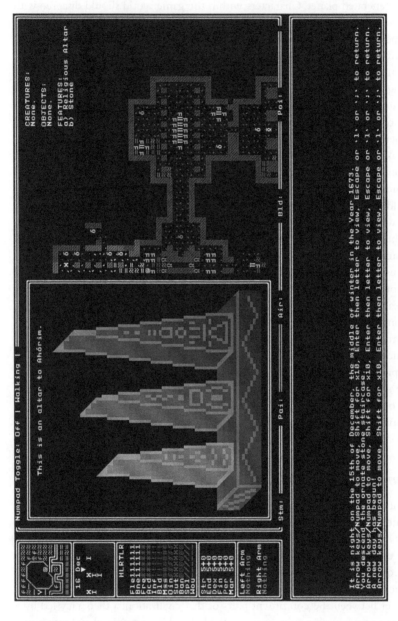

FIGURE 6.4 The player examines a procedurally generated religious altar within a subterranean crypt deep below the desert

cultural life of that nation); and a chiefdom, where a single powerful individual rules without the same system of vassalage as a monarchy. In every case, as with everything else, these are procedurally generated. For example, if a nation emerges as a democratic society, the game will make a judgment about how to distribute seats within its parliament – based on land area, towns, wealth, colonies, or whatever else – in a way which seems convincing and sensible. This means some democratic societies are controlled by the rich and powerful, while others are closer to a "true" democracy and less vested in the interests of the most influential. Alternatively, if the government is a monarchic, the game will generate titles for this monarch, logical and appropriate to the cultural or geographical settings: a monarch near the poles might be "Lord of the Ice", or one near the desert might be the "Scorpion Queen", and so on. In turn, each of these governmental options influences how the people of that nation behave to strangers, such as the player, and what sorts of buildings and characters appear; sure enough, the player will find delegates in democratic nations, lords in monarchic nations, and powerful priests in theocratic ones. These political choices are both constructed from the ground up in the philosophies and histories of each generated nation and reverberate down through the world in as many ways as possible.

Religions and Ideologies (Political)

Alongside these different governmental norms and their associated physical infra-structures, URR is also replete with procedurally generated religions, and each of these religions comes with its own set of manifestations and political agendas. Every belief system has a procedurally generated holy book or series of books (which adherents might quote), a set of edicts and expectations, different moral codes, different styles of clothing, and different perspectives on how nonbeliev-ers should be treated. A particularly zealous religion might be the most likely to send preachers to different cities (to potentially be encountered by the player) or send inquisitors throughout their own territory to find potential heretics. These are characters the player might meet on their travels, and these are the sorts of characters who will be woven into the stories and histories of appropriate cul-tures; perhaps an inquisitor accused a great ruler of heresy, and the ruler was sub-sequently toppled, but all of that only happened because that particular religion in that particular location was especially concerned by doctrinal accuracy, and their interactions and relationships with the other moving pieces in the world all emerged organically. Equally, some religions will emphasize, or ban, certain kinds of weapons or certain sorts of equipment. For example, a religion might believe that heavy weapons such as maces should not be used because they do too much damage to human bodies (which are perhaps sacred?) and thus no soldiers following that religion will use these weapons. In turn, that will affect their role in armies they serve in, it will affect books written about or paintings drawn of these soldiers, it might change how other soldiers think about them, it will shift how well the player can integrate with that religion should they choose to, and so a seemingly trivial thing like a choice of weapon is designed to bring about far-reaching effects within the generated world. The proscription against heavy weapons is not merely a little piece of world-building detail, and nor is it an arbitrary gameplay requirement, but rather a political edict which is designed to resonate throughout the world and its history.

Faces and Appearance (Social)

Moving into the more "social" dimensions of world-building, it was important for me to reflect in the game the diversity of people we see in the real world. The generated faces of characters within the game can take on any one of several million possible forms. Faces vary in terms of skin tone and eye color, the former of which equates roughly to latitude, while genetic groups of eye color and their geographical distribution are generated randomly when a new world is created. Hair color works in the same way with genetic distributions being different in each created planet, thereby sometimes generating combinations which tend not to appear in the real world. Hair styles, meanwhile, are socially determined, with each civilization having a small number for women, and a small number for men, which are considered socially acceptable. Although some of these elements are genetic rather than social, even the genetic elements are designed to be integrated with gameplay: encountering individuals very clearly from a different part of the world is meant to tell the player something about them, as potential travelers, traders, diplomats, and the like. Equally, some characters the player encounters might judge them based on their appearance, while others will not. Alongside these genetic and cultural elements of facial generation and their integration with how the player communicates with (and learns about) other characters, there are many other aspects of how nonplayer characters (NPCs) look. Some cultures will perform facial tattooing or scarification, or wear turbans or necklaces or jewelry of various sorts. Again, the importance here was that people in the game should look distinct, and their appearance should give the player hints as to their backgrounds; their faces should be tied to their geography, their cultures, and their personal lives. This is all part of the game's sociological world-building: the construction of a world of diverse cultures, who are distinct from each other, interact with each other, and which can be learned and understood through the player's exploration.

Clothing and Style (Social)

Alongside these differences in facial appearance which integrate world-building into gameplay and generate world-building elements which resonate in many different contexts, the clothing styles of different characters are also an essential element of social world-building. Once again, the goal was not to create clothing styles which exist in a vacuum, but rather clothing styles which seem appropriate to the climates, cultures, and technological knowhow from which they originate. The majority of the civilizations in the game are akin to the European or Asian states of the time period in question, which is to say large, sedentary societies with clearly defined territories, distributions of labor, and so forth. Their clothing is procedurally generated from a vast number of potential permutations, with further variation on the individual level according to the weight of a character and their social status or rank (Figure 6.5). Nomadic nations, which occupy some of each generated world's deserts, opt for lighter, looser clothing, more suited to long travels by horse and the heat of their homelands: again, each culture has its own style, but all styles are recognizable to the experienced player as belonging to a nomadic culture. Characters from tribal nations, meanwhile, portray a range of potential dresses, again distinct from the other categories of clothing as a whole, but also each culture's clothing is distinct from the others. There are also unique clothing styles for each and every religion – which are different from another one, but still broadly within a clear, overall larger category – and the styles of armor and weaponry are different for every culture, who craft them in specialized ways (yet still in ways similar to their other clothing: same colors, same shapes, and so forth). Given all this variation, nonplayer characters respond in profoundly different ways depending on what the player character wears, and so understanding the in-game cultural associations of each item or rank of clothing is essential to the player's navigation of complex social situations. In all cases the goal was the same: to further distinguish cultural groups from one another, to enable the player – and other characters – to make judgments about characters based on their clothing and also allow for deception and disguise as a gameplay mechanic. In this way, the clothing styles are not just a question of detail but also an aspect of world-building, further fleshing out the richness of each world and its people.

Dialects and Naming (Social)

The third social element of world-building I sought to build into *URR* was linguistic world-building. In this regard, I was not especially interested in generating entire fictional languages. I debated this at length, but no digital game has ever really found a convincing and interesting system to have a player "learn" an invented language, and I also found this just as challenging to figure out as game designers before me. Instead, however, I was interested in the idea of dialects, something almost never seen in other games (although accents are sometimes present in voice acting). In-game characters from different cultures speak in dialects, and every one of these dialects is procedurally generated. When a world is created, the game crafts new ways for people from a certain culture to speak, and then later when generating any sentence – including those written in books – will use these dialect choices to ensure consistency. As the player, talking to another character will generate lines of dialogue in the appropriate dialect, allowing the player to gradually come to associate each dialect with its own culture. Some cultures

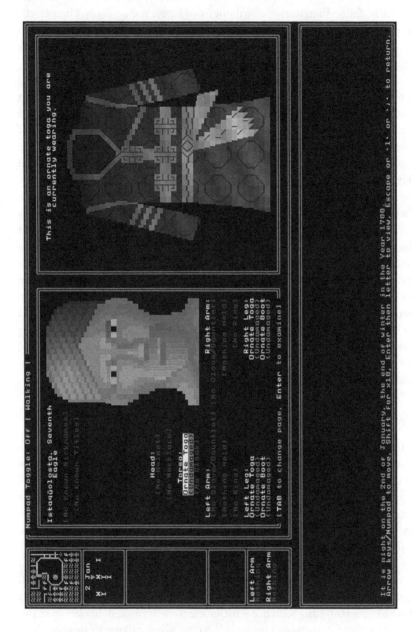

FIGURE 6.5 A procedurally generated player character, wearing their generated item of well-tailored clothing

will be derogatory toward how other cultures speak, which affects interactions between characters including the player; in turn, the player can learn to mask their dialect by speaking another dialect, as a means to infiltrate other cultures. This commitment to cultural differences in speech patterns is also found in how names are created for each civilization. The game has around 50 archetypes of names, but then each archetype can either be altered randomly, or altered according to the rest of the game world, drawing on ideas like animals or plants to create a set of possible names. Once again, when the player learns a style of naming, they should be able to identify the origin of another character and then make informed choices on the back of that information.

Currencies and Values (Economic)

Moving now to economic world-building, the creation of a functioning and convincing in-world economy has always been one of the rarest elements of world-building, even in games where currencies are often important elements of gameplay. Think about the ubiquity of "gold" as a currency in many fictional premodern worlds, or the ubiquity of "credits" in futuristic world. How were these single currencies agreed upon, and why are these currencies so different from those in the real world, with their varied designs, reissuing of coins or notes, inflation, deflation, and so forth? These ideas inevitably tie everyone into a single economy, and as the real world has shown – most visibly in the uneven uptake of the euro within the EU – even close allies and closely linked economies do not always believe it to be in their self-interest to share a currency. Equally, despite its inherent appeal, auric coinage has actually been relatively rare in the history of the real world: even historically, many of the most effective and long-lived currencies were not based on gold, and in the present day, it is only specialist nonnational coinages, such as Krugerrands, which continue to use gold in their manufacture. Instead, in *URR*, every nation has its own currency made of different metals (or in rarer cases, nonmetal materials), and its coinage has a unique shape, a unique design, and is traded at a particular value with the currencies of other nations. Some nations impose tariffs, while others do not. Coinage uses symbols meaningful to the civilization in question, while some currencies are more or less valued than others due to the nations that guarantee their value: this, in turn, reflects what currencies people want to trade in. Currencies are therefore not a single unified "neat" thing in the worlds of *URR*, but varied, emergent, and integrated with other elements of the world. More broadly, with these six elements of world-building alongside many others described here, the goal has always been twofold: to create a world which is less obvious and less transparent than many fictional worlds, and to use bottom-up sociological world-building to build a planet which is not just a complex set of interwoven elements, but also different every time a player creates a new world – yet always one that is, hopefully, as deep as the one which came before it.

Conclusions

In this essay, I have sought to look at how political, social, and economic world-building might manifest itself in digital games. World-building is, of course, a vast and diverse practice in digital games, let alone in all creative media. Nevertheless, I propose this kind of world-building tends to be relatively rare compared to others (such as the geographical, the linguistic, the mythological) and yet is essential to creating a world which seems to truly function as an internally consistent fictional space. Of course, this is not to say that many classic pieces of world-building – both in games and beyond – have not generated huge success, visibility, influence on later world-builders, and significant profit for their creators. Yet, as I hope I have shown here, there is immense potential for fictional worlds, for gameplay, for storytelling, and much else, by exploring the possibilities of the bottom-up sociological construction of convincing fictional worlds. The cultural and social complexities of the real world are not built from the top by an objective and rational hand, but from the bottom by many millions throughout history, and that is how we should build our fictional worlds too.

References

Fairburn, M., *Social History: Problems, Strategies and Methods*, Basingstoke: Macmillan International Higher Education, 1999.

Fass, P. S., "Cultural History/Social History: Some Reflections on a Continuing Dialogue", *Journal of Social History*, 37 (1), 2003, pp. 39–46.

Furumoto, L., "Beyond Great Men and Great Ideas: History of Psychology in Sociocultural Context", in P. Bronstein and K. Quina, editors, *Teaching Gender and Multicultural Awareness: Resources for the Psychology Classroom*, Washington, DC: American Psychological Association, 2003, pp. 113–124.

Gilmore, M., "George R. R. Martin: The Rolling Stone Interview", *Rolling Stone*, April 23, 2014, available at www.rollingstone.com/culture/culture-news/george-r-r-martin-the-rolling-stone-interview-242487/.

Goodfellow, C., and Cybulski, A., "Capitalist Dogs, Attack Squids and Telepathic Defectors: Science Fiction Video Games and the Cybernetic Imagination in the USA and Russia", Canadian Game Studies Association Annual Conference, 2016.

Grinblat, J., and Bucklew, C. B., "Subverting Historical Cause & Effect: Generation of Mythic Biographies in Caves of Qud", Proceedings of the 12th International Conference on the Foundations of Digital Games, ACM, August 2017, p. 76.

Gunn, S., "From Hegemony to Governmentality: Changing Conceptions of Power in Social History", *Journal of Social History*, 39 (3), 2006, pp. 705–720.

Johnson, M. R., "Alternate History Aesthetics in Red Alert. *Memory Insufficient*", 2015, available at http://meminsf.silverstringmedia.com/art/alternate-history-aesthetics-in-red-alert/.

Johnson, M. R., *The Unpredictability of Gameplay*, New York and London: Bloomsbury Academic, 2018.

Kaiser, R., "Europa Universalis Review", *IGN*, August 15, 2013, available at https://ca.ign.com/articles/2013/08/15/europa-universalis-iv-review.

Karth, I., "Preliminary Poetics of Procedural Generation in Games", Proceedings of the Digital Games Research Association, 2018.

Lucy, J. A., *Language Diversity and Thought: A Reformulation of the Linguistic Relativity Hypothesis*, Cambridge: Cambridge University Press, 1992.

Parkin, S., "Bloodborne Creator Hidetaka Miyazaki: 'I Didn't Have a Dream. I Wasn't Ambitious'", *The Guardian*, March 31, 2015, available at www.theguardian.com/technology/2015/mar/31/bloodborne-dark-souls-creator-hidetaka-miyazaki-interview.

Roine, H. R., *Imaginative, Immersive and Interactive Engagements. The Rhetoric of Worldbuilding in Contemporary Speculative Fiction*, Ph.D. Thesis, 2016.

Salge, C., Green, M. C., Canaan, R., and Togelius, J., "Generative Design in Minecraft (GDMC): Settlement Generation Competition", Proceedings of the 13th International Conference on the Foundations of Digital Games, ACM, August 2018, p. 49.

Vella, D., "No Mastery Without Mystery: Dark Souls and the Ludic Sublime", *Game Studies*, 15 (1), 2015, available at http://gamestudies.org/1501/articles/vella.

Walker, J., "I Really Wanted to Be Able to Play Stellaris", *Rock Paper Shotgun*, May 16, 2016, available at www.rockpapershotgun.com/2016/05/16/i-really-wanted-to-be-able-to-play-stellaris/.

Wolff, P., and Holmes, K. J., "Linguistic Relativity", *Wiley Interdisciplinary Reviews: Cognitive Science*, 2 (3), 2011, pp. 253–265.

Young, P., *Globalization and the Great Exhibition: The Victorian New World Order*, Basingstoke: Palgrave Macmillan, 2009.

7

CONCERNING THE "SUB" IN "SUBCREATION"

The Act of Creating Under

Mark J. P. Wolf

As a Roman Catholic philologist who was increasingly aware of the philosophical implications of his writing and world-building, J. R. R. Tolkien made the distinction early on between the kind of creation that human authors and world-builders do, and God's *ex nihilo* (from nothing) creation. Human beings, created in the image of God, also have a desire to create, but such creative activity differs in both degree and kind from *ex nihilo* creative power, since it uses the existing concepts and ideas found in our world (the "Primary World") and recombines them in the building of an imaginary (or "secondary") world; thus, human creation is "creating under" or in Tolkien's term, "subcreating", within God's creation. A secondary world, then relies on the Primary World for its raw materials as well as for whatever elements and features make it able to be understood by, and related to, an audience. And because invention in a secondary world resets Primary World defaults, a secondary world relies on Primary World defaults for anything that is not specifically replaced or reinvented within the secondary world.

So secondary worlds, then, can be seen as versions of the Primary World in which things have been added, subtracted, or changed, and the more changes are made, the more invention occurs, and the more "secondary" the world becomes. When enough is changed, we have what appears to be a new world, different from our own, an imaginary world. This, of course, raises the question, just how different can a secondary world be from the Primary World? To what degree can subcreating be done? If one were to try to subcreate a world with as *little* reliance on Primary World defaults as possible, how far could one go, and what might such a world be like? While designing an imaginary world, couldn't one simply keep locating Primary World defaults and changing them, until no such defaults remain?

To begin the exploration of the extreme reaches of subcreative possibility, we could start with the various levels of invention which I have written about else-where, the *nominal, cultural, natural,* and *ontological*.[1] Invention which changes the *nominal* realm merely gives new names to existing things; taken to an extreme, this is essentially the making of a new language, which renames existing things. Although it has the potential to cast a new light on the things it names, by empha-sizing certain aspects about them or relating them to each in new ways through linguistic similarities, the level of actual invention is somewhat shallow compared to the other levels.

Invention which changes the *cultural* realm deals with all things made by humans (or other creatures) and in which new objects, artifacts, technologies, customs, institutions, ideas, and so forth appear. Much subcreation falls within this realm and is what allows a secondary world depicted in audiovisual media to have a distinct appearance and style, including costumes, art, architecture, vehicles, food, technology, and so forth, and distinct sounds as well (like the hum of lightsabers in the *Star Wars* galaxy or the sound of the transporter beam in the *Star Trek* galaxy). Invented terms can also indicate new cultural concepts, such as J. R. R. Tolkien's "mathom" or Philip K. Dick's "kipple".[2] Since a wide range of cultural designs and artifacts can be found in the Primary World, there is a great latitude for inven-tion, especially when one considers that even in the Primary World, such things need not be practical or necessary in order to exist.

Beyond the *cultural* realm, invention in the *natural* realm changes nature itself and includes new landmasses, planets, plants and animals, entire ecosystems, and other aspects of the natural world itself which are changed or invented by an author. Invention in the natural realm will often still rely on designs or conven-tions found in the Primary World; for example, a unicorn is an invented animal, but its appearance is like that of a horse, except for its single horn. New plants and animals are usually based on combined features of existing plants and animals, so as to give them plausible zoological or biological explanations. On a larger scale, inventions may include new planetary forms, such as the worlds of Larry Niven's *Ringworld* series or Terry Pratchett's *Discworld* series, which have planets shaped like rings and discs, respectively. Although elements of the natural world are changed at this level, the resulting inventions are still usually designed so that their existence might be considered plausible within the universe we know.

The next level, the *ontological* realm, determines the parameters of a world's existence —that is, the materiality and laws of physics, space, time, and so forth that constitute the world and which can differ from the universe of the Primary World. For example, the worlds of Edwin Abbott Abbott's *Flatland* (1884) and A. K. Dewd-ney's *The Planiverse* (1984) are both set in universes with only two spatial dimen-sions, which automatically make them quite different from the universe of three spatial dimensions in which we live. Such worlds, though very different from our own, are still often connected in some way to the Primary World, whether through portals, communication technologies, or other devices or conventions; and much of their content is similar, though often by analogy. Alan Lightman's *Einstein's Dreams* (1992), for example, features vignettes of universes in which time and space behave differently, reflecting philosophically on each one, and together they are connected to our world as a series of dreams that Einstein has while working on his theories. Some common science-fiction conventions, including faster-than-light travel, other dimensions, time travel, and wormholes used for interstellar travel usually imply laws of physics that are different than those currently understood, though the full consequences of such differences are sometimes not carried out in the design of the worlds that use them. Because the consequences of ontological changes are so vast and all-encompassing, relatively few worlds are subcreated at this depth to the degree they could be; many choose to simply use conventions as accepted solutions for problems like space travel over long distances.

Changes on the natural and even ontological levels are possible due to the way familiar concepts can be recombined. Tolkien noted that the separation of adjectives and nouns made this possible in literature:

> When we can take green from grass, blue from heaven, and red from blood, we have already an enchanter's power – upon one plane; and the desire to wield that power in the world external to our minds awakes. It does not follow that we shall use that power well upon any plane. We may put a deadly green on a man's face and produce a horror; we may make the rare and terrible blue moon to shine; or we may cause woods to spring with silver leaves and rams to wear fleeces of gold, and put hot fire into the belly of the cold worm. But in such "fantasy", as it is called, new form is made. . . . Man becomes a sub-creator.[3]

Authors subcreating in the ontological realm can go even farther than combining colors with objects, using the concept of color itself to create new colors that do not exist in the Primary World, such as "jale" and "ulfire" (due to the blue sun in David Lindsay's *A Voyage to Arcturus* (1920)); "rej" in Philip K. Dick's *Galactic Pot-Healer* (1969); or "octarine", the "color of magic" in Terry Pratchett's *Discworld* universe. Some colors may not be given a name; as Raymond King Cummings writes in *The Girl in the Golden Atom* (1922), "Her lips were full and of a color for which in English there is no name. It would have been red doubtless by sunlight in the world above, but here in this silver light of phosphorescence, the color red, as we see it, was impossible".[4] Naturally, all of these new colors occur in novels rather than audiovisual media, since they would otherwise have to actually be visualized. Other worlds that have different laws of physics are also best left to nonvisual media, such as the world of Greg Egan's *The Clockwork Rocket* (2011) where light has no universal speed. On the other hand, some films visually depict such things like travel through other dimensions, as in *Doctor Strange* (2016), while some video game worlds let players experience alternative physical laws, like the negative gravity in some of the "universes" in *Gravitar* (1982), the non-Euclidean wraparound space of *Asteroids* (1979), or the user-generated spatial connections of *Portal* (2007).

But all these worlds, different as they may be, are still worlds in which stories are set. In worlds where many of the Primary World defaults have been changed, even at the natural and ontological levels, there are still a number of connections and similarities to the Primary World that a secondary world must retain in order to be a successful vehicle for stories which engage audiences and remain a place to which they can still relate in some manner.

Secondary Worlds and Storytelling

As more and more Primary World defaults are changed in the realms just described, the resulting secondary worlds grow ever farther away from the Primary World in similarity, leading one to ask what the minimum requirements are for a world, if it is still to contain compelling stories which are relatable to audiences. These elements are reducible to four elements necessary for relatability: structures and experiences which are analogous to those of the Primary World; plausible cause-and-effect relationships; a moral dimension to choices, behavior, and outcomes; and emotional realism.

The first of these four elements lays the groundwork for the other three. In order for a narrative to be relatable, it must be analogous to Primary World experiences so that audiences have some way to map the narrative onto their own experiences. We can relate to characters like Luke Skywalker or Frodo Baggins because we can find similarities in their experiences to our own, even though their worlds differ greatly from ours. Even nonanthropomorphic characters and the stories told about them can become engaging and relatable, if enough analogous connections exist – for example, the lives of the rabbits in Richard Adams's *Watership Down* (1972) or all the animals in Beatrix Potter stories. One could even tell stories about diaphanous gasbag creatures that live in the atmospheric layers of Jupiter; coming-of-age stories about younger gasbags leaving their parents, stories of courtship and reproduction, conflicts of warring groups competing with each other for resources or territory, and stories of sacrifice and loss as lives end. Physically, such creatures and their environment are far from anything like human beings on Earth, yet socially and emotionally, there may be enough analogous experience to keep an audience engaged, though bringing out the similarities that create the analogies may be difficult. Thus, many such fantastic stories rely on conventions and narrative tropes to make themselves relatable, sometimes resulting in stories that are too well known and overdone. We might refer to these basic requirements for such analogies as *space*, *time*, and *character*; in other words, *someone* who is *somewhere* doing *something*. Or, more particularly, *beings* living in an *environment* using *resources*, from which some kind of narrative goal or conflict can develop. For these to develop, we need the second element: plausible cause-and-effect relationships.

Causality, connecting actions and their consequences in predictable, repeatable ways, allows characters to exhibit teleological behavior and work toward goals; one has to have some sense of what consequences one's actions will have if one is to plan to accomplish anything. These connections should also be plausible, at least within the world's own ontological rules and laws of physics, even if they are different from those of the Primary World; we might accept that a space station's superlaser can cause a planet to completely explode (as opposed to merely burning a hole through it, as one might more reasonably expect), but we are not likely, even in the most outlandish science fiction story, to accept a handheld gun that is able to destroy a whole galaxy with one shot.[5] Cause-and-effect relationships presume physical laws of some kind, and spatial and temporal dimensions in which actions occur and cause reactions and other kinds of consequences. Again, these can be quite different than those of the Primary World, but they are conceptually similar. A. K. Dewdney's Planiverse has only two spatial dimensions, which change the nature of wave dissipation through space; sound, light, and gravity diminish less over distances because they are spreading within a two-dimensional space instead of a three-dimensional space.[6] The concept of wave dissipation, however, remains the same, and the same mathematics are applied to both the Primary World and the secondary world of the Planiverse, and as a result, predictable behaviors, and causality, remain. Of course, causality often cannot entirely explain the actions of sentient beings, and characters can be so different that they are not understood by the audience or other human characters in the secondary world. A good example of this is the sentient ocean in Stanisław Lem's *Solaris* (1961), which the story's scientists know is intelligent even though they are unable to find a way to communicate with it, even by the novel's end.

A predictable set of plausible cause-and-effect relationships not only means that characters can plan ahead, guessing the outcomes of their actions, but that characters can choose actions with either more desirable or less desirable outcomes or even outcomes which hurt other characters. Thus, we come to the third element: a moral dimension to choices, behavior, and outcomes. Without a sense of right and wrong, characters' actions would have no meaning, and stories would have no purpose. Scottish author George MacDonald recognized this in "The Fantastic Imagination", the Introduction to *The Light Princess and other Fairy Tales* (1893), where he examined how laws are used to form an internally consistent imaginary world, and the role of moral laws within one as well:

> The natural world has its laws, and no man must interfere with them in the way of presentment any more than in the way of use; but they themselves may suggest laws of other kinds, and man may, if he pleases, invent a little world of his own, with its own laws; for there is that in him which delights in calling up new forms – which is the nearest, perhaps, he can come to creation. When such forms are new embodiments of old truths, we call them products of the Imagination; when they are mere inventions, however

lovely, I should call them the work of Fancy; in either case, Law has been diligently at work.

His world once invented, the highest law that comes next into play is, that there shall be harmony between the laws by which the new world has begun to exist; and in the process of his creation, the inventor must hold by those laws. The moment he forgets one of them, he makes the story, by its own postulates, incredible. To be able to live a moment in an imagined world, we must see the laws of its existence obeyed. Those broken, we fall out of it. The imagination in us, whose exercise is essential to the most temporary submission to the imagination of another, immediately, with the disappearance of Law, ceases to act. . . . A man's inventions may be stupid or clever, but if he does not hold by the laws of them, or if he makes one law jar with another, he contradicts himself as an inventor, he is no artist. He does not rightly consort his instruments, or he tunes them in different keys. . . . Obeying law, the maker works like his creator; not obeying law, he is such a fool as heaps a pile of stones and calls it a church.

In the moral world it is different: there a man may clothe in new forms, and for this employ his imagination freely, but he must invent nothing. He may not, for any purpose, turn its laws upside down. He must not meddle with the relations of live souls. The laws of the spirit man must hold, alike in this world and in any world he may invent. It were no offence to suppose a world in which everything repelled instead of attracted the things around it; it would be wicked to write a tale representing a man it called good as always doing bad things, or a man it called bad as always doing good things: the notion itself is absolutely lawless. In physical things a man may invent; in moral things he must obey – and take their laws with him into his invented world as well.[7]

Wicked though it may be, it is possible "to write a tale representing a man it called good as always doing bad things, or a man it called bad as always doing good things", but even in such a story, there is still a sense of right and wrong, even if the characters' notions of them disagree with right and wrong as understood by the audience. Characters can have a faulty moral compass or act lawlessly, but the notions of right and wrong still exist in the secondary world and are even what make such things possible. It means that what characters do matters. Likewise, outcomes are also valued as good or bad and affect the meaning of the story, character arcs, and how the audience responds to the story.

Finally, emotional realism is built on all the other elements and determines to what degree the emotions felt by the characters will be shared by the audience who identify with them. Emotions may have different or new forms of expression or even be suppressed (as with *Star Trek*'s Vulcans), but they must be present to some degree in character interactions to evoke empathy or sympathy. A character's actions and reactions must be solidly based on his or her emotional makeup; the more we know about the character, the more nuanced their emotional states need to be. If we do not feel that the character is acting as we would act in a similar situation, identification may become lessened or even lost; instead, we may even grow angry that the character is making choices which seem foolish or stupid and thus consider the character, and perhaps even the story, unrealistic – or at least badly written. While many other implausible elements are accepted – some perhaps grudgingly, simply because the audience likes the characters or the world – a lack of emotional realism will leave an audience cold and without an emotional connection to the world or its action.

Most imaginary worlds exist because they are the settings in which the author's stories are told, so a story's success or failure often means success or failure for the world as well. In many cases, the world is only there to support the story, and world-building is a background activity, allowing storytelling to remain in the foreground of the audience's experience. At times, however, world-building may overtake storytelling. In worlds designed primarily for entertainment (like James Cameron's Pandora in *Avatar* (2009)), for satirical purposes (like Samuel Butler's Erewhon), for the purpose of scientific speculation (like A. K. Dewdney's *Planiverse*), or for thought experiments of a philosophical nature (like those of Alan Lightman's *Einstein's Dreams* (1992)) or a political or social nature (like Thomas More's Utopia), exposition regarding the peculiarities of a secondary world can completely overtake narrative, reducing it to little more than a frame story. In many video games, narrative also becomes a way of providing context for the games' action and is relatively thin and simple, compared to the richly detailed three-dimensional worlds where many games now take place.

So what if a world-builder is not all that concerned about whether a story works emotionally, or whether it works at all? Or even if there is any story at all? Video games, for example, can give a player a detailed, immersive sandbox-style world to wander around in, with little or no preplanned narrative, and as long as the world is interesting, this won't even bother many players. Even when a preplanned story is available, a player may ignore it just to wander around the world, as in *Grand Theft Auto V* (2013), where players can forego the game's missions to simply roam about the world, stealing cars and other vehicles, getting into police chases, and generally creating their own narrative material as they interact with the world. Of course, this then becomes a replacement narrative of sorts, but one can also just wander around as an observer, with little or no concern for the absence of a storyline.

Secondary Worlds Beyond Storytelling

Once we eliminate the requirements for a narrative as described previously, we are free to replace even more world defaults, subcreating even further away from the Primary World template. We may have stories which no longer are as engaging, with characters like the sentient ocean of Solaris, whom we cannot understand or relate to, and perhaps even cause-and-effect relationships are abstracted to such a degree that they are bewildering. Or perhaps there is really no story or narrative structure at all, just information about a world.

Without a narrative, a work depicting a world can be structured as a collection of smaller texts, like an encyclopedia or an atlas, or even something more experimental, like Luigi Serafini's *Codex Seraphinianus* (1981), a profusely illustrated 360-page book written in an untranslated made-up language that is designed to look like a scientific treatise describing the flora, fauna, inventions, and civilizations of an unnamed imaginary world. With an unreadable text, one can only browse and speculate, and the book's many strange and whimsical images do not entirely come together to suggest a complete and consistent world on their own, which appears to be part of the author's design, since speculation plays such a large part of the experience of the book.

At this point in the journey into deeper and deeper subcreating, the nature of the world defaults being changed also begins to change. Most of the changes described in the previous section involve the material, physical aspects of the world, and sometimes additional concepts, but leave much of the Primary World's *conceptual* realm intact. We may see a wide variety of vehicles and weapons in science fiction, but the conceptual categories of *vehicles* and *weapons* remain the same and help the audience relate to the world. Even in the *Codex Seraphinianus*, conceptual categories from the Primary World (such as *plant, animal, food, clothing,* and *shelter*) still remain in use and give many of the book's images the little relatability that they have. In order to subcreate even further away from the Primary World, the changed defaults, then, must move from the physical and perceptual realm into the conceptual realm, and the *Codex* does this in some places, by providing objects which appear to blur the boundaries of conceptual categories: creatures that appear to be part plant, part animal, and part vehicle (with wheels growing out of them) and other objects with no apparent use or Primary World analogs. Events are also depicted which have no clear purpose and which mix beings, machines, and raw materials together in ways that make them difficult to categorize. This is a good part of the book's creativity; the images, which are forced to stand on their own due to the unintelligible text, seem like they are often deliberately designed to cross conceptual boundaries and try to present things which are as startlingly inexplicable as possible. Yet many drawings hint at or contain recognizable bits and pieces from the Primary World – an eyeball here, part of an alligator head there, droplets of liquid transforming into something else – enough for the book to still be engaging visually, regardless of the viewer's own cultural background.

Our next step, then, would be to try to subcreate a world like that of the *Codex*, but one in which we remove even those little details that come from the Primary World, as well as any conceptual categories that indicate purpose, function, and use, or even such binary oppositions as *animate* versus *inanimate*. We could eliminate all written text and make all the imagery appear entirely abstract (at least from a human point of view), even though it would be, at the same time, completely representative of the world being depicted. But would a book or film made up of such imagery even be identifiable as a world? We get brief glimpses of such places in films like *2001: A Space Odyssey* (1968) and *Doctor Strange* (2016) when their main characters fly through interdimensional portals and are surrounded by patterns of light and colorful, moving abstractions representing other worlds beyond what we know. The weirdness and unexplainedness of these places is exactly what the filmmaker wants, to disorient the audience as much as possible and show something which is not understandable. But these are relatively brief glimpses, and we still have a main character passing through who is a human, and the alien intelligences contacting the human characters in both films give them recognizable things to work with; in *2001*, David Bowman finds himself in a strange bedroom with Louis XVI décor and Renaissance sculptures and paintings, while Doctor Strange lands and walks on a planetary surface and Dormammu, ruler of the "Dark Dimension", appears to him as an anthropomorphic face and converses with him in English. A world without such connections, without recognizable objects or narrative material, completely unfamiliar and abstract (to us) would be hard to maintain longer than a glimpse, and would we even be able to recognize it as a world?

Hitting the Glass Ceiling of Subcreative Possibilities

At this point, it becomes increasingly difficult to identify and continue changing the remaining Primary World defaults, either because we do not know what to change them to, or because we are not even fully aware of them all, having taken them for granted as the only possible way something can be. It is sometimes said that mathematics must be the same in all parts of the universe, which makes it a possible bridge to alien cultures, being something we would share in common with them.[8] Some theorists even go so far as to say that mathematics would have to be the same *in any universe*, regardless of how different that universe is from our own, but this says more about our ability to conceptualize than it does about math. Just because we cannot conceptualize or imagine something does not mean that it cannot exist; it would be rather arrogant to suggest that the universe must be limited to containing only those things which human beings are able to detect, understand, or imagine.

If we are depicting an imaginary world, then we still have default concepts such as *beings* (or in authorial terms, *characters*) who exist within a *time* and *space*. We could drop the idea of characters, imagining an empty universe devoid of any sentient beings, similar to the early universe before life existed within it. But the notions of *space* and *time* do seem to be particularly hard to do without; we can reduce space to two dimensions or even to one, but even lines and points are always depicted as having some visible form, instead of the infinitesimally small and featureless mathematical objects that they are supposed to be. Likewise, we can imagine different types of time, or configurations of variations of time, running at different speeds, or backward, but there is always some idea of time involved (even frozen time), just as depictions of points and lines always take up some amount of actual space, instead of being infinitesimally small. What it would be like to have *no* space or *no* time is simply unimaginable to beings like us familiar only with spatiotemporal existence.

Theologically speaking, as the Creator of the universe and of the space and time that make it up, God is not subject to space and time, and exists outside their bounds.[9] Angels, devils (which are fallen angels), departed souls, Heaven, and Hell likewise exist outside the spatiotemporal universe we live in, existing in what we sometimes refer to as the eternal. Yet we cannot help imagining even these things as existing within spatiotemporal dimensions; the eternal is imagined as time that just keeps on continuing, and heaven and hell as places which angels or devils are depicted occupying in crowds, along with the souls of the departed. They are, for the most part, depicted as extensions of the only existence we know, but in extreme degrees and durations.

Although we can posit these things and imagine being outside of time and space, exactly what that means or what it would be like is beyond our grasp, limited as we are to our current spatiotemporal existence. Try as we might, we can only imagine such things by way of analogy, reflecting on our experience in the Primary World. Even if we can recognize the concepts of *time* and *space* and *matter* and *energy* (the last two of which are really two forms of the same thing, as Einstein showed) as defaults that are not necessary to Creation (that is to say, God could create a universe without them), we cannot imagine what the alternatives might be. Not only can we not create *ex nihilo* the way God can, then, but we are limited to create within – or "under" – the current universe in which we live, and our own creations will always necessarily reflect those limitations to some extent. (At least while we are still here on Earth; if the subcreative urge in human beings is one way in which we are created in the image of God, as Tolkien supposed, then perhaps we will be given new subcreative abilities in the afterlife, something which Tolkien suggests by way of analogy in his short story "Leaf by Niggle" (1945), which ends with Niggle finding the unfinished painting he was working on complete and no longer just an image but an actual world.)

Currently, however, we are inevitably limited in how far we are able to subcreate a secondary world. Far from lamenting our limitations, though, we should be more appreciative of just how amazingly far we *can* go; most worlds still fall short of what can be done, and we have just begun in earnest to scratch the surface of possible worlds and their construction. Of course, some secondary worlds will always be closer to the Primary World in their design, and not all worlds need to be subcreated into the ontological realm in order to convey their ideas or stories. But it is good to know the possibilities are there.

The subcreational act of world-building involves not only making choices between options but also being aware of what options are available, and sometimes the latter can be more difficult than the former. Awareness of defaults, and how they can be changed, necessarily precedes advancements of any kind, be they technological, cultural, or social ones. A healthy subcreative urge can also keep us aware of the possibilities available to us in the Primary World, for its own reshaping, and keep us from falling prey to fatalism and despair, and that alone makes for a better world.

Notes

An earlier version of this essay appeared in for *Sub-creating Arda: World-building in J. R. R. Tolkien's Work, Its Precursors, and Its Legacies*, edited by Dimitra Fimi and Thomas Honegger, Zollikofen, Switzerland: Walking Tree Publishers, 2019, pages 1-15, and I would like to thank the editors for allowing me to reprint it here.

1. See Mark J. P. Wolf, *Building Imaginary Worlds: The Theory and History of Subcreation*, New York: Routledge, 2012, pp. 35–37.
2. Tolkien wrote, "anything that Hobbits had no immediate use for, but were unwilling to throw away, they called a *mathom*" (J. R. R. Tolkien, *The Lord of the Rings*, paperback One-Volume Edition, Boston and New York: Houghton Mifflin Company, 1994, p. 5); while Dick wrote, "Kipple is useless objects, like junk mail or match folders after you use the last match or gum wrappers or yesterday's homeopape. When nobody's around, kipple reproduces itself" (Philip K. Dick, *Do Androids Dream of Electric Sheep* (originally published in 1968), New York: Ballantine Books, 1990, p. 57).
3. From J. R. R. Tolkien, "On Fairy-stories", in Verlyn Flieger and Douglas A. Anderson, editors, *Tolkien On Fairy-stories*, London: HarperCollins, pp. 41–42.
4. Raymond King Cummings, "Chapter XIX. The City of Arite", *The Girl in the Golden Atom*, first serialized in *All Story* magazine in 1919, and then published as a novel in 1922.
5. The superlaser reference is, of course, referring to the Death Star space stations of the *Star Wars* galaxy. Since the diameter of the superlaser beam appears to be smaller than a city, at least, one would expect it to drill a hole through a planet-sized body, yet the planets it strikes explode as if made entirely of flammable materials.
6. See A. K. Dewdney, *The Planiverse: Computer Contact with a Two-Dimensional World*, New York: Copernicus, an imprint of Springer-Verlag, 2001, p. 110.
7. From "The Fantastic Imagination", The Introduction to George MacDonald's *The Light Princess and Other Fairy Tales* (1893), reprinted in *The Heart of George MacDonald*, Rolland Hein, editor, Vancouver, British Columbia: Regent College Publishing, 1994, pp. 424–425.
8. See, for example, Martin Rees, "Mathematics: The Only True Universal Language", *New Scientist*, February 11, 2009, available at www.newscientist.com/article/mg20126951-800-mathematics-the-only-true-universal-language/.
9. Religious belief is not necessary for speculations as to what is "outside" the universe we know; for example, the Many-Worlds Interpretation of Quantum Theory, a form of which was first posited by Hugh Everett in 1957, suggests myriads of parallel universes with alternate histories and futures.

APPENDIX

Types of World-Building

What exactly do we mean by the "world" in "world-building"? The question seems an obvious one, since it refers to the imaginary world in question which one is building or adding to. But the nature of such additions varies, as does their relationship to the world in question, and "world-building" can be narrowly or broadly applied as well. I have written elsewhere about what I have called the "circles of authorship" involved in the making of imaginary worlds, but here I will focus instead on the status of the content being added to a world, rather than authorship itself.[1] In this sense, we can divide the world-building that has to do with a particular world into seven categories, which we can also conceptualize as concentric circles, moving from the center outward: world origination, diegetic material, extradiegetic material, paratetxual material, translations and adaptations, the completion of world gestalten, and noncanonical extensions.

World Origination

The originator of a world, the world's author, begins the world by coming up with the characters, locations, relationships, and so forth, usually in the form of the first narrative to be set in that world; typically, this narrative and the world are developed together. This work forms the conceptual basis of the world, its ontological rules, its backstory, and so forth. Although world origination could be done by committee, there is usually a single person who is the main originator and who has the initial idea for the world.

Diegetic Material

The diegesis of a narrative work is defined as everything that is a part of the world, everything that the world's characters can see and hear. Along with world origination, the creation of this kind of material is the most commonly used meaning of "world-building", as it directly builds the imaginary world in some way. This includes the actual production of the elements of a world, or their assembly (as in the case of visual effects compositors who composite visual effects elements together, but do not make them), as well as the overseeing and approval of those producing them or the decision-making which decides which elements or designs will be used. The diegetic material of a world is usually the main thing that we think of when discussing the world itself.

Extradiegetic Material

The extradiegetic material includes things the characters cannot see or hear; in film, these would include the main title sequence and end credits, the voiceover of a narrator, the musical soundtrack, and subtitles or intertitles; in literature, it would include chapter titles and cover art; in video games, title screens, credit screens, save screens, nondiegetic tutorials, and so forth. Thus, extradiegetic material is arguably not part of a world in the strictest sense, since the characters cannot sense these things at all; they are not part of the secondary world's existence.

But the presentation of world data and information is not always so clear cut. In novels, for example, there may be maps, glossaries, time lines, and other sources of canonical information which arranges that information into a document for the reader, even though the document is not available to or known by the characters with the world. The Appendices found at the end of *The Lord of the Rings* (1954–1955), for example, is a part of the novel, yet not a diegetic part, though the timeline relates many diegetic events; it presents diegetic information but in a more distanced way than does the text of the story itself.

It also seems wrong to claim that, for example, John Williams's music for *Star Wars* is not a part of that world. And indeed, some of his music is, in fact, diegetic, like the Cantina Band music, which the characters hear as well as the audience. But should the *Star Wars* main title theme be considered a part of the world? I would argue that it is an important part of *the audience's experience of a world*, which is usually included in what we mean by a "world"; for to what degree can a secondary world be said to exist if no one ever experiences it? If we broaden the definition of "world-building" to include the audience's experience of a world, we can include extradiegetical material (and the other remaining categories, if we choose), and consider all the things by which a world is known, such as the *Star Wars* font used in the opening title or the "A long time ago in a galaxy far, far away . . ." opening narration title; these are all part of the experience that surrounds a vicarious journey into the world of *Star Wars*, at least as far as the films are concerned.

We may even suggest, then, that just as there is a sense of canonicity for the diegetic elements, there can be an author-approved "official" canon of extradiegetic elements, like the ones just discussed for *Star Wars*. Thus, an author who designs his or her own book cover could claim it to be the official cover, as opposed to other cover designs that appear on later printings of the book. Since the extradiegetic materials are closely tied to the diegetic ones (and indeed, may even be hardly separable from them, due to the mediated nature of presenting imaginary worlds), one could argue that the world's author ought to also have control over the extradiegetic materials, since they also determine the audience's experience of the world. This varies, however, from one medium to another; movie directors usually do have a say in title fonts and musical soundtracks, whereas a book's author may have no say in the cover design of the book. This brings us to the marketing of a world and the works in which it appears, over which an author may have limited or even no control.

Paratextual Material

Literary theorist Gérard Genette defined "paratext" as things that accompany a text, including a preface, introduction, illustrations, and index, and even the author's name. By his definition, paratexts are extradiegetic materials, but he was writing about literature and not media in general. Since "paratext" suggests something alongside (or parallel to) a text, we will use the broader meaning of the term often found in media studies, where it refers to other whole texts that run alongside a main text. By using this definition, we can separate extradiegetic material (which is a part of a work along with diegetic material) from paratextual material (which appears in other separate works alongside the main ones composed of diegetic and extradiegetic material. By this definition, then, "paratexts" would include movie posters, visual guides, companions, "making of" documentaries, atlases, and so forth. Though such works are mainly for audiences who want to know more about the world and its making, these works can occasionally reveal additional canonical diegetic material – for example, *Star Wars Mythmaking: Behind the Scenes of 'Attack of the Clones'* (2002) contains photographs of sets like the Dexter's Diner and the freighter interior, revealing details that were not seen (or could only be glimpsed) in the film itself. It is precisely such additional information that may encourage the sales of such works, for fans eager to know more about a world, particularly trivia that may not be well known in general.[2]

Paratextual material can also reveal the making of a world and the earlier stages of an author's world-building. The "making of" documentaries made for movies often reveal production designs, including early and even discarded ones. Christopher Tolkien's 12-volume *History of Middle-earth* series contains early drafts of his father's writings, revealing J. R. R. Tolkien's working methods. Christopher Tolkien also edited and published *The Silmarillion* (1977) after his father's death in 1973. Since the works within *The Silmarillion* were not published or released by J. R. R. Tolkien himself, who was still working on them at the time of his death, one could question whether the elder Tolkien had considered them close enough to their final form to be considered canonical; at the same time, Christopher Tolkien, as his father's literary executor, certainly had the authority to publish the works.

While paratextual material can add canonical material to a world, it is generally less important material as regards the narratives set in the world, though that can change as a world grows and more stories are added. But the remaining three areas to be examined can arguably be considered world-building despite that fact that they do not add any canonical material to the world in question.

Translations and Adaptations

As worlds spread, they become translated into other languages and adapted into other media. These processes inevitably add new material; movies visualize what is only described in books, and translations can subtly alter a text, or even outright change the words of an invented language (like Tore Zetterholm's Swedish translation of *The Hobbit* (1937), which inexplicably changed "hobbit" to "hompen" and "Bilbo" to "Bimbo"). Without the participation or approval of the world's creator, no new additions or visualizations can be considered canonical; they would only be what we could call interpretations of a work. When Peter Jackson made a three-film adaptation of *The Lord of the Rings* (2001–2003), the resulting images and designs were only one possible visual interpretation of the novel, and some of them even differ somewhat from Tolkien's own illustrations created for his stories. In cases where there are multiple adaptations of a novel and its world into a movie (like the multiple adaptations of Frank Herbert's *Dune* (1965)), one can see the variety and range of possibilities for such interpretations.

Even though interpretations and adaptations do not add canonical material, they greatly affect the experience of a world, especially if the audience is unfamiliar with the original source material. Oftentimes interpretations are gateways to a world, and the audience members' first encounter with a world, and so a misleading first impression due to a mediocre or bad translation or adaptation could turn away interest in a world, before the original is ever encountered, resulting most likely in the original never receiving the attention it might have otherwise. On the other hand, good world-building in an adaptation can bring in audiences that may not have been interested in the original work; novels that are from another era can be updated and made more appealing to a contemporary audience (for example, Robert Paltock's novel *The Life and Adventures of Peter Wilkins* (1750) could easily be made into an effects-laden film spectacle). So even though nothing canonical is added, adaptations can contain a great deal of world-building and can affect the visibility, popularity, and reputation of a world.

Completion of World Gestalten

The completion of world gestalten occurs when one fills in the missing details of a world based on assumptions made from real-world defaults or extrapolations of existing secondary world infrastructures or data. We might guess what a building looks like based on the building style of a fictional culture or figure out the meaning of a word in a constructed language based on other words of the language, and so on. Each person will fill gaps and complete world gestalten in their own idiosyncratic way, for just themselves, as opposed to an interpretation or adaptation, where one person completes such gaps, but the results are presented to an audience. Such gap-filling can be even be done automatically without a person's thinking about it; one simply makes assumptions about how to fill in missing pieces, and the more a person is certain about what is to be filled in, the more likely it is the person will not even need to be aware of the conscious choice involved in filling it in.

Although the results of such gap-filling is strictly kept, for the most part, in the mind of the audience member, this can still be considered a form of world-building, because it takes an inevitably incomplete world and fills in details that make the world seem more complete and more real. Because it differs from one audience member to the next, this is perhaps not often considered as actual world-building, especially since the results are not experienced beyond the individual involved. But it still needs to be considered by the world's originator and main world-builders, since how someone completes world gestalten depends on what details they are given, whether verbally, visually, or otherwise. World-builders, then, must determine what to tell or show the audience, what to leave to their imagination, and what details will lead to what assumptions. And, of course, assumptions and expectations can be played with, as horror movies have so successfully shown; mystery and speculation can likewise make a world more appealing. Thus, even the completion of world gestalten can be seen as a form of world-building which has an effect on the audience's experience of a world.

The completion of world gestalten can occur automatically or be done consciously by the audience, in the form of speculation, and taken to an extreme, audiences may even begin to fill in entire stories about minor characters, side events, or even new stories about a world's main characters and events. At this point, they are creating fan fiction, which we could also refer to as noncanonical extensions.

Noncanonical Extensions

Fan fiction is a form of world-building that extends a world but which adds nothing canonical to it, and unlike interpretation or adaptation, it adds new stories using existing characters, locations, objects, and so on. One can take several attitudes regarding such extensions. One is that fan fiction is a form of imitation and flattery performed by fans who enjoy the world enough to want to participate in the making of stories that take place there. On the other hand, one could consider it a very lazy, derivative (or even parasitic) form of world-building, with fans using other people's characters and settings and so forth instead of putting forth the effort required to try to invent their own. Either way, the secondary world being extended has been successful enough to ignite the desire for world-building in its audience, which is a sign of a successful world and one which people enjoy inhabiting vicariously.

The term "world-building", then, is used to describe a variety of very different activities, from world origination to the completion of world gestalten. Although all these do contain some form of world-building to warrant the term, one must be careful not to lump them all together, as they are quite different in kind and in the overall effect they have on a world. Not all of them add canonical material, some are more limited in their effects than others, and the efforts involved and skills required in each differ greatly as well.

And yet, all of these activities do effect people's experience of a world, so they are all things that can be taken into consideration whenever a new secondary world is built, for it is not just the content of the world itself, but the overall experience of the audience that encounters the world, that determines much of its success.

Notes

1. See Chapter Seven, "Circles of Authorship", in Mark J. P. Wolf, editor, *Building Imaginary Worlds: The Theory and History of Subcreation*, New York: Routledge, 2012.
2. See Jody Duncan, *Star Wars Mythmaking: Behind the Scenes of 'Attack of the Clones'*, New York: Del Rey Books, 2002, pp. 70, 71–74, 76–77, 107.

ABOUT THE CONTRIBUTORS

Richard A. Bartle is Honorary Professor of Computer Game Design at the University of Essex. He is best known for having cowritten in 1978 the first virtual world, *MUD*, and for his 1996 player types model, which has seen widespread adoption by the MMO industry. His 2003 book, *Designing Virtual Worlds*, is the standard text on the subject, and he is an influential writer on all aspects of MMO design and development. In 2010, he was the first recipient of the prestigious GDC Online Game Legend award. [richard@mud.co.uk]

Clara Fernández-Vara is Associate Arts Professor at the NYU Game Center. She is a game scholar, designer, and writer. Her main research interest is the study and creation of narrative games and how they create worlds in which the player can perform. Clara's digital media work is grounded in the humanities, informed by her background in literature, film, and theater. Her book, *Introduction to Game Analysis* (Routledge, 2014), is now in its second edition. [clara.fernandez@nyu.edu]

Tracy Fullerton is an experimental game designer, professor, and director emeritus of the USC Games program. Her research center, the Game Innovation Lab, has produced several influential independent games, including *Cloud* (2005); *flOw* (2006); *Darfur is Dying* (2006); *The Night Journey* (2007) with artist Bill Viola; and *Walden, a game* (2017), a simulation of Henry David Thoreau's experiment at Walden Pond, which was named "Game of the Year" at Games for Change 2017 and "Developer Choice" at IndieCade 2017. Tracy is the author of *Game Design Workshop: A Playcentric Approach to Creating Innovative Games* (2004, 2008, 2014), a design textbook used at game programs worldwide, and holder of the Electronic Arts Endowed Chair in Interactive Entertainment. Prior to USC, she designed games for companies including Microsoft, Sony, and MTV, among many others. Tracy's work has received numerous honors, including an Emmy nomination for interactive television, Indiecade's "Sublime Experience", "Impact", and "Trailblazer" awards, the Games for Change "Game Changer" award, the Game Developers Choice "Ambassador" Award, and *Time Magazine's* Best of the Web.

Henry Jenkins is Provost's Professor of Communication, Journalism, Cinematic Arts, and Education at the University of Southern California and the founder and former codirector of the Comparative Media Studies Program at MIT. He is the author or editor of more than 20 books, including *Textual Poachers: Television Fans and Participatory Culture* (1992), *Convergence Culture: Where Old and New Media Collide* (2006), and the forthcoming *Comics and Stuff* (2020). He blogs at henryjenkins.org and cohosts the *How Do You Like It So Far?* podcast. [hjenkins@usc.edu]

Mark R. Johnson is Lecturer in Digital Cultures in the Department of Media and Communications at the University of Sydney. His research focuses on the intersections of play and money, such as live streaming, e-sports, gamification, gamblification, and playbor. He has published in journals including *Information, Communication and Society*, *Convergence*, *Media, Culture and Society*, and *Games and Culture*, while his first monograph, *The Unpredictability of Gameplay* (Bloomsbury, 2018), proposes a new Deleuzean framework for understanding unpredictability in digital games. He is also the independent game developer of the world-building/roguelike game *Ultima Ratio Regum*, a retired professional poker player, and a regular games blogger and podcaster. [markrjohnsongames@gmail.com]

Alex McDowell, RDI, is an award-winning designer and storyteller working at the intersection of emergent technologies and experiential media. Until 2012, McDowell was a production designer, with 30 years of experience in feature films, working with directors David Fincher, Steven Spielberg, Terry Gilliam, and Anthony Minghella, among others. He was the production designer for *Fear and Loathing in Las Vegas* (1998), *Man of Steel* (2013), *Watchmen* (2009), *Charlie and the Chocolate Factory* (2005), *Fight Club* (1999), and *Minority Report* (2002). His production design work on *Minority Report* (2002) is considered seminal both for its vision of near-future technology and its integration with people's behavior and is believed to have resulted in nearly 100 patents for new technologies. He is now Professor of Practice in Media Arts + Practice at USC School of Cinematic Arts, where he teaches world-building. He is director of the USC World Building Media Lab (WbML), where McDowell and his interdisciplinary students build immersive worlds for storytelling and narrative design practice across multiple platforms. The lab's research has been featured at the Sundance New Frontier and at CES. Currently the lab has formed a partnership with the USC Bridge Institute, which has yielded a unique art-science team who are collaborating in the development of a new visual language for the Pancreatic Beta Cell. The WbML was awarded the prestigious Future Voice Award at the 2014 Interaction

Awards in Amsterdam. McDowell also leads the USC World Building Institute, a renowned cross-media knowledge space. He is the recipient, from George Lucas, of the William Cameron Menzies Endowed Chair in Production Design. He is director of the World Building Institute, which, among other events, curates a three-day workshop annually at the Berlinale International Film Festival. He is the cofounder of Experimental, a narrative design studio where he and his expert team are applying their skills to crafting immersive story worlds for major industries and institutions. As Visiting Artist to the MIT Media Lab (2005–2010), he designed the robot opera *Death and the Powers* (2010). He is a Getty Research Institute scholar, a member of the Academy of Motion Pictures Design Branch, and an executive board member of the Academy of Motion Pictures Sci-Tech Council. He is on the boards of the UK Government's Arts and Humanities Research Council and the international Pancreatic Beta Cell Consortium. In 2006, he was awarded Royal Designer for Industry by the UK's Royal Society of Arts and, in 2013, was given the UK Designers & Art Directors' President's Award. [alex@experimental.design]

Mark Sebanc is an independent scholar, editor, translator, and novelist. He holds a bachelor and a master of arts in classics from the University of Toronto and lives with his Costa Rican wife in the Upper Ottawa Valley of Ontario, Canada. He is coauthor, with James G. Anderson, of *The Stoneholding* (2009) and *Darkling Fields of Arvon* (2010), the first two installments of "The Legacy of the Stone Harp" epic fantasy series, projected to run to five novels. Both titles are published by Baen Books. [marksebanc@gmail.com]

Matthew Weise is a game designer whose work spans industry and academia. He is the CEO of Empathy Box, a company that specializes in narrative design for games and across media. He was the narrative designer at Harmonix Music Systems on *Fantasia: Music Evolved* (2014), the game design director of the GAMBIT Game Lab at MIT, and a consultant for Warner Bros., Microsoft, Eko, PBS, The National Ballet of Spain, and others on storytelling and game design. His work, both creatively and critically, focuses on transmedia adaptation with an emphasis on the challenges of adapting cinema into video games. Matt has given lectures and workshops on film-to-game adaptation all over the world and has published work on how franchises like *Alien*, James Bond, and horror cinema in general are adapted into games. Links to his writing and game design work, including his IGF-nominated *The Snowfield* (2011), can be found at www.matthewweise.com. [sajon@mit.edu]

Mark J. P. Wolf is Professor in the Communication Department at Concordia University, Wisconsin. He has a BA (1990) in film production and an MA (1992) and a PhD (1995) in critical studies from the School of Cinema/Television (now renamed the School of Cinematic Arts) at the University of Southern California.

His books include *Abstracting Reality: Art, Communication, and Cognition in the Digital Age* (2000), *The Medium of the Video Game* (2001), *Virtual Morality: Morals, Ethics, and New Media* (2003), *The Video Game Theory Reader* (2003), *The Video Game Explosion: A History from PONG to PlayStation and Beyond* (2007), *The Video Game Theory Reader 2* (2008), *Myst and Riven: The World of the D'ni* (2011), *Before the Crash: Early Video Game History* (2012), *Encyclopedia of Video Games: The Culture, Technology, and Art of Gaming* (two-volume First Edition, 2012; three-volume Second Edition, forthcoming), *Building Imaginary Worlds: The Theory and History of Subcreation* (2012), *The Routledge Companion to Video Game Studies* (2014), *LEGO Studies: Examining the Building Blocks of a Transmedial Phenomenon* (2014), *Video Games Around the World* (2015), the four-volume *Video Games and Gaming Cultures* (2016), *Revisiting Imaginary Worlds: A Subcreation Studies Anthology* (2017), *Video Games FAQ* (2017), *The World of Mister Rogers' Neighborhood* (2017), *The Routledge Companion to Imaginary Worlds* (2017), *The Routledge Companion to Media Technology and Obsolescence* (2018), *Exploring Imaginary Worlds: Essays on Media, Structure, and Subcreation* (forthcoming), and two novels for which he is looking for a publisher. He is also the founder and coeditor of the Landmark Video Game book series from University of Michigan Press, the founder and editor of the Imaginary Worlds book series from Routledge, and the founder of the Video Game Studies Scholarly Interest Group and the Transmedia Studies Special Interest Group within the Society of Cinema and Media Studies. He has been invited to speak in North America, South America, Europe, Asia, and Second Life; has had work published in journals including *Compar(a)ison, Convergence, Film Quarterly, Games and Culture, New Review of Film and Television Studies, Projections,* and *The Velvet Light Trap;* is on the advisory boards of Videotopia, the International Arcade Museum Library, and the *International Journal of Gaming and Computer-Mediated Simulations;* and is on several editorial boards, including those of *Games and Culture* and *The Journal of E-media Studies.* He lives in Wisconsin with his wife, Diane, and his sons Michael, Christian, and Francis. [mark.wolf@cuw.edu]

INDEX